SHERBROOKE STREET

A collection of important Canadian reprints
edited by John Metcalf and John Newlove

1. *The Improved Binoculars,* Irving Layton

2. *Cape Breton is the Thought-Control Centre of Canada,*
   Ray Smith

3. *Lunar Attractions,* Clark Blaise

4. *Europe,* Louis Dudek

Europe

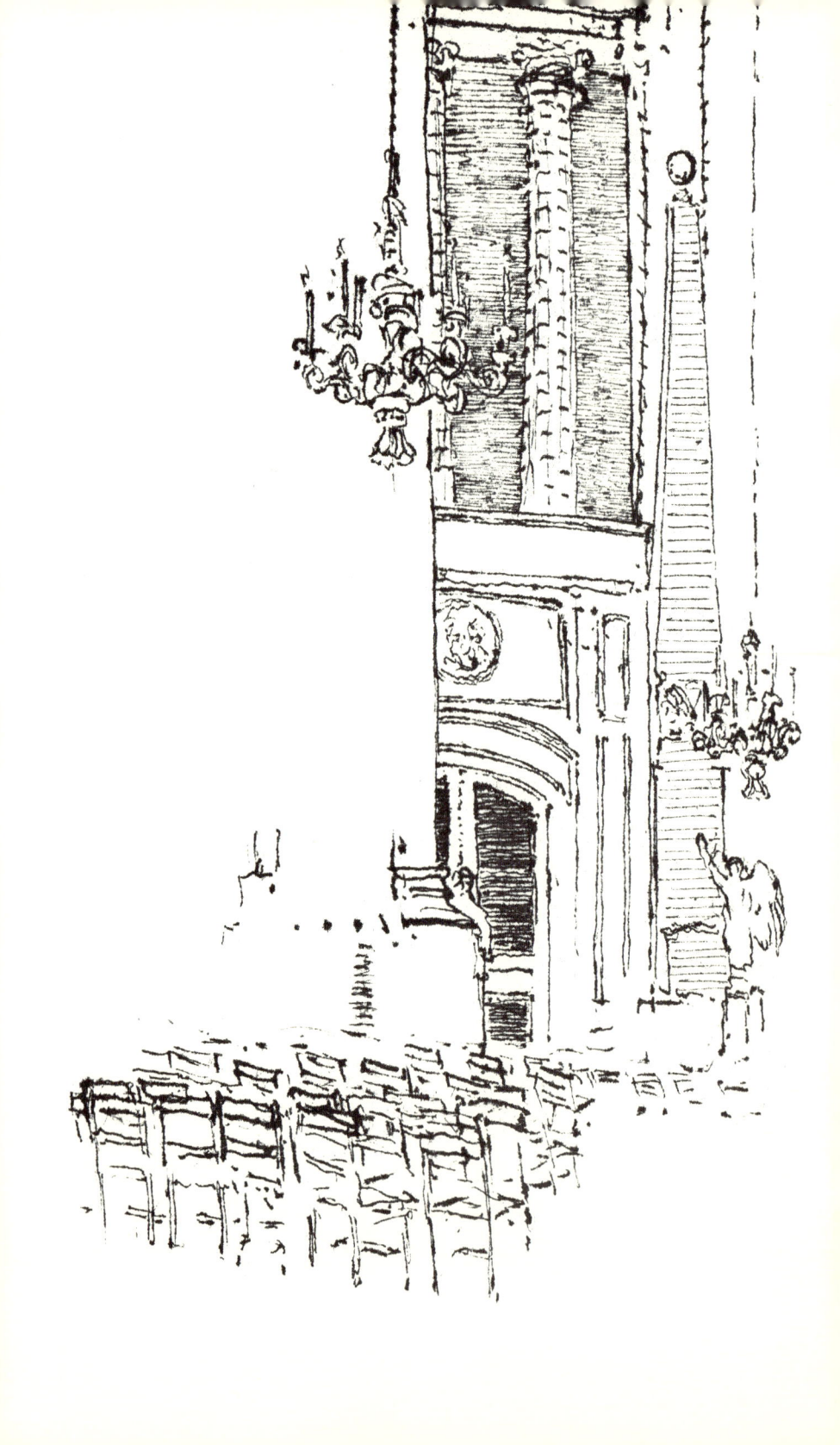

Europe

Louis Dudek

Revised
According to the Original Manuscript
with Emendations

and a new Afterword
by Michael Gnarowski

The Porcupine's Quill

CANADIAN CATALOGUING IN PUBLICATION DATA

Dudek, Louis, 1918-
　Europe

(Sherbrooke Street ; 4)
Rev. according to the original manuscript with emendations and a new afterword / by Michael Gnarowski.
ISBN 0-88984-115-2

I. Gnarowski, Michael, 1934- .　II. Title.
III. Series.

PS8507.U43E6 1991　　C811'.54　　C91-094051-7
PR9199.2.D8E6 1991

Copyright © Louis Dudek, 1991.

Published by The Porcupine's Quill, Inc., 68 Main Street, Erin, Ontario N0B 1T0 with financial assistance from The Canada Council and the Ontario Arts Council. Originally published by Contact Press (1954).

Distributed by The University of Toronto Press, 5201 Dufferin Street, Downsview, Ontario M5H 5T8.

Edited for the press by John Metcalf.

The cover is after a photograph of the Cathedral at Bourges, taken by Tony Urquhart. All interior art is also by Tony Urquhart.

Printed and bound by The Porcupine's Quill, Inc.
The stock is Zephyr laid, and the type, Ehrhardt.

for Stephanie
who shared it

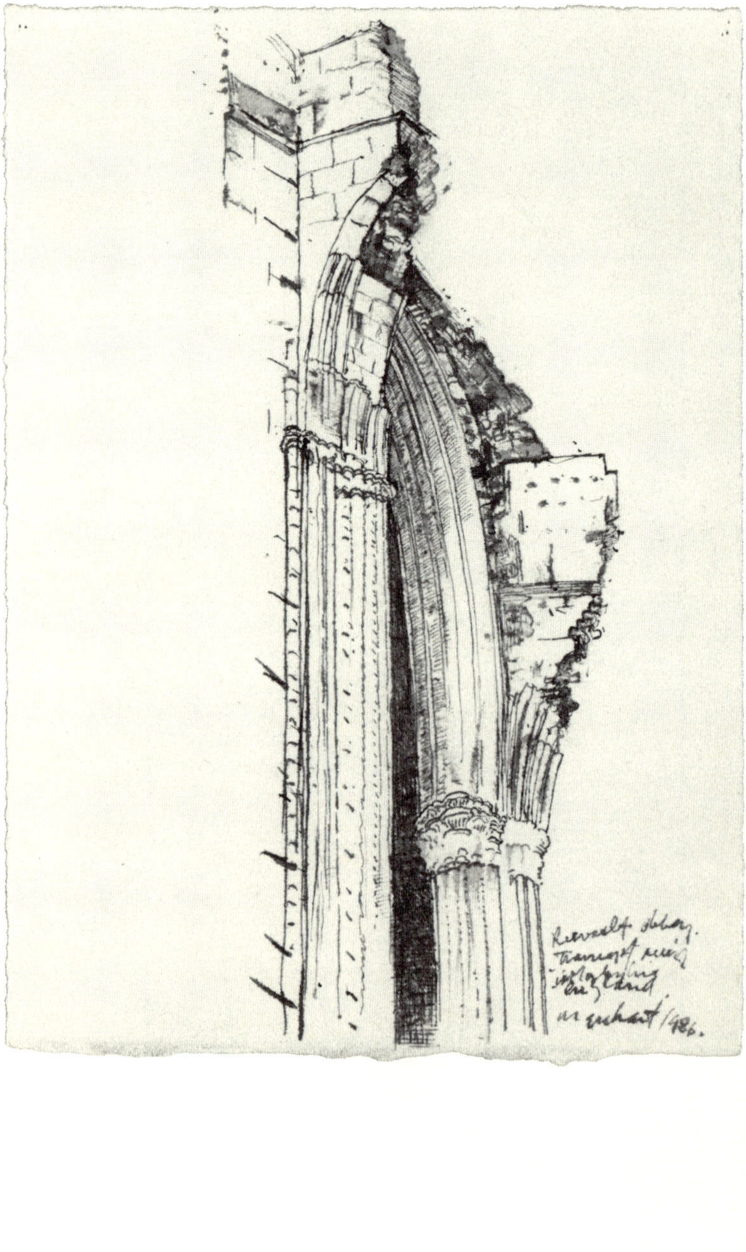

Preface

It's very difficult for me to write about a poem I wrote more than thirty-five years ago when I was a young man. But at least I can say that the poem still moves me, and carries me along in its sweep, as I reread and edit the text.

And yes, I stand behind every word of it, behind every line, as I read what that young man has written – despite the arrogance and vehemence which were then reproved as 'didacticism'.

The views expressed, I should add, are not ideological. I was never a party man, or an adherent of any ideology, Marxist, Poundist (Social Credit), or socialist, for that matter. Democracy, yes, humanity and justice. But that is the extent of my commitment.

Ideas may come from various sources, but observations are primary. It is the search for truth, one's own personal forging of the truth, that is at stake, and that moves through this poem and on into other long and short poems.

When I look at architecture or paintings in Europe, it is what I see and reflect upon in my own way that enters into the poem, not the writings of historians and art critics. Teachers try to persuade the young to respond and think for themselves, yet as adults we seem to be unable to recognize and allow this freedom in others.

How much one suffers for thinking freely, in one's own way! And yet poetry requires nothing less – it requires the most absolute independence of the individual.

Similarly, when I refer in my poems to philosophers and political thinkers (or other poets), it is not to echo their ideas, but rather because I have thought much and long, in my solitudes, using their thoughts as props and occasional gleams to illuminate the darkness. I want to see the world as for the first time, for myself. Hence the arrogance, and also innocence, of this early poetry.

As I go back to the poem, I now realize there were developments in my life, and in Canadian poetry at the time, that bear very much on what I wrote.

The first that comes to mind is that I was then (in 1953) just beginning to teach a course in European literature, for which I had prepared at Columbia University in New York. Professor Algy Noad at McGill had died recently, and I was to continue his course of lectures 'The Great Writings of Europe.' It had been a highly restricted and specialized course, requiring a knowledge of languages; but I made it a study of literature in translation, a reading of the major writers and thinkers from the eighteenth century to the present, and that in their most disturbing and radical implications. A kind of down-going of the west. A look at what is happening out there in Europe. So it became a course in the history of ideas, a study of the disintegration of belief and of social coherence in western society from Voltaire and Rousseau to Louis Ferdinand Céline, Sartre, and Samuel Beckett.

When the violence of the sixties broke out on the campuses, I ceased to teach this course, feeling that my warnings to my students had been futile and that the fanaticism and anarchy about which I had lectured – and which I dreaded – had now exploded in our midst. The prophecies of Dostoevsky, Turgenev, Nietzsche had been fulfilled, even in Canada.

The book *Europe* in some ways reflects the readings I had been doing for that course. I find among my papers a page of quotations, intended to be used as epigraphs for the poem, with the note in ink, 'Place before *Europe* in reprinting (as originally intended),' and these are obviously things I had picked up in my reading.

The way these epigraphs are ordered and presented appears to be virtually an outline of the poem's thematic concerns, though it was put together after the poem was completed of course. (The shape of a poem comes together, by ways strange and mysterious, as the poem is being written, not from an outline prepared beforehand.)

Here are the epigraphs, with their title (which is crossed out in the original):

A Kind of Resumé

'Heureux qui, comme Ulysse, a fait un beau voyage ...'
Du Bellay

'Aux fortunes du monde ai-je droit de toucher?
Ai-je un pied sûr et ferme, et qui puisse marcher
Dans ce sentier, semé de ruines vandales ...'
Victor Hugo

'Beer-bottle on the statue's pediment!
That, Fritz, is the era, today against the past,
Contemporary.'   *Ezra Pound*

'Commercio alto gridar, gridar commercio ...'
Parini

'Rien de certain parmi les anciens, rien de beau parmi les modernes.'   *Chateaubriand*

'To build the city of Dioce whose terraces are the colour of stars.'   *Ezra Pound*

Another influence on the poem is the experience of my New York years. I had come back to Montreal in 1951 after an absence of seven years (with summer visits to Montreal), studying history and comparative literature at Columbia. The key figure here is Emery Neff, whose books *A Revolution in European Poetry* and *Carlyle and Mill,* and whose seminars, had given me much of the European background for the Romantic period. A.H. Thorndike's *Literature in a Changing Age* was also an important source. (Add to this that Professor Evans, in History, had lectured in mediaeval history; and Westermann, who appears in the poem, in ancient history. John Brebner, a Canadian historian, was also my tutor in British history. So all these studies, as well as others at Columbia, are somewhat reflected in the poem.)

They are, of course, not responsible for the content of my ideas, for as I have said above, these are generated in the light of experience, and are highly personal.

For the Modern period, I attended very demanding seminars under Lionel Trilling and Jacques Barzun, though I never found any great affinity with either of these scholars. Also, I attended lectures by Mark Van Doren and by William York Tyndall, as well as one public lecture by Alexander Kerensky, early leader of the Russian Revolution; and of course listened to numerous poets at the YMHA poetry readings organized by Kimon Friar. (T.S. Eliot, Wallace Stevens, William Carlos Williams stand out as vivid memories.)

The Trilling/Barzun seminar involved me further in the study of the profession of letters, which had already been the subject of my MA in history, under Brebner, and which I had brought with me as an obsession from Montreal. This culminated in the dissertation, and later the book, *Literature and the Press*, which was being completed and published concurrently with the poem *Europe*. The subject is probably crucial to the poem.

>Genoa is greasy and full of business
>of the kind already familiar,
>   except that the old streets
>are still as narrow
>as when they built San Lorenzo,
>and they do sell
>   Pindemonte's Omero
>   at half a dollar.
>Though we have come here to see old Europe,

> it is the new which really concerns us,
>   here as in America.
> The past speaks in the remaining monuments
>   and a few pages
>   of the dead poets,
> judging the Esso empire
> and the new Milanese
>   without mercy.

The vehemence of my indignations in the poem, and the serenity which the sea provides, as a background, has much to do with my view of the writer in the modern world. On the whole I see the author reduced to a degraded position, brought to impotence by commercial and technological developments; and this has to do with the general degradation of civilized values that accompanies the evolution of historical ideas from about 1750 to the present, that is, the content of 'The Great Writings of Europe.'

Even Ezra Pound disagreed with my view of Genoa, because my point of view differed very much from his. He roared that I should 'study some history.' (The letter seems to be missing from the book *Dk/Some Letters of Ezra Pound*; I assume there must be a letter lost.)

In other words, if you know enough about the background of this subject, and if you are involved in the concerns that appear in the best thinkers, you will find nothing surprising in the drive and hortatory passion of this poem. It is only one form of expression, or response to the reality, which one would expect from any mind involved in the tragedy of modern history.

Other developments which were in progress at the time of this poem include the activity around the magazine *CIV/n* and the beginnings of Contact Press, in collaboration with Raymond Souster and Irving Layton. We had published the three-poet book *Cerberus* in 1952, in which I say that reality is 'a metaphor made of iron', and that poetry is 'the epic that all men would live if they were free.' Reality is a metaphor made of iron because reality imposes itself upon us and sometimes breaks us, while poetry imagines a possible future, and is always open with a naïve spontaneity to life.

This bears on the poem *Europe*, since the sea makes and unmakes all reality like its own dissolving waves. The openness of this poem, in human terms, also relates me to the poetry of Souster, which I have always loved and admired, despite the fact that my subject is so much more far-ranging and perhaps scholarly than anything he would have preferred.

Cid Corman, on the other hand, did not like the poem, saying it was good enough as a private diary but not much more. No surprise then, that I on my part have never been sympathetic to the poetry in *Origin* – Olson et al. – which to me seemed angular, external, and devoid of close personal feeling. These are different worlds.

Of course, if you return to those years you return to the turbulence and controversy of actual life. The poetry is outside and above all that.

CIV/n was the magazine we then produced, edited by Aileen Collins, assisted by her friends. We were all for freedom and adventure in ideas and in poetry, argument and discussion were an important ingredient in that company. So when I completed the poem I read the whole thing through to 'the children of light' – Irving and Betty Layton, Aileen Collins, Jackie Gallagher, Buddy and Wanda Rozynski, and perhaps a few others – assembled in Layton's parlour, in the rickety house on Kildare Road. Jackie Gallagher actually fell asleep during the reading, which is not at all surprising, since it's a long and exhausting poem for one sitting. I cannot now imagine where I found the incredible gall to put a group through that kind of ordeal. And yet the fact that I did so is itself a measure of the enthusiasm and the exhilaration that I felt at the time. *Europe* was an ecstasy, and so it remains for me – as I hope it will be for many readers.

The three great subjects of the poem, its thematic vehicles, are of course the Sea, the Cathedrals, and the Acropolis of

Athens. I write them in capitals, since they are symbolic bearers of a larger meaning, each a different dimension of the great possibility. (Like the epigraphs, ending with 'the city of Dioce', they are the themes of some redeeming good, either in the past, or in eternity, or yet again in the ever-living present.)

On the back of one of the manuscript worksheets (that for Poem 58) I find a suggestive title outline for the parts of the book, a set of titles that was abandoned, but which indicates an organizational direction for the idea:

I	The River
II	Sea
III	Island
IV	Continent
V	Epilogue.

In other words, the parts of the poem – which finally became less indicative, simply geographical – 'I Sea and Land', 'II England', 'III France', 'IV The Warm South', 'V What Greece Has Given', and 'Finis' – could be seen as representing this abstract progression which was first jotted down. The tendency to raise the organization to an abstract order is typical of the human mind: one hypothesis is that this is a search for the order that really inheres in things. But there are other ways of seeing it.

The in-and-out of abstraction is what the poem demonstrates. And this problem leads to the strains of organization and disorganization, of idea and pure perception, that continue through my later poetry.

What matters is the emotion that carries the poem along, emotion generated by perceptions and ideas flowing together. These are the creative elements.

'Like the dead, we remember
the symbolic events that mattered ...

*

a priest on a bicycle; the Italian girls on the train
who said with their eyes that 'love
is better than money'; the young man in the church
at Lancaster, and the woman who prayed
in Mainz: all these are remembered
in the first effort to return, to relive in memory
what was too little comprehended. Life, like poetry,
can only be understood through comparison, what results
is the perfect, unchanging essence,
        an eidolon of the good.

        *

The sea retains such images
        in her ever-unchanging waves;
for all her infinite variety, and the forms,
inexhaustible, of her loves,
she is constant always in beauty,
        which to us need be nothing more
than a harmony with the wave on which we move....

   'Eidolon', a word from Whitman – 'Passing the hues and objects of the world, / The fields of art and learning, pleasure, sense, / To glean eidólons' – here means 'the image of an ideal conception' (from the Greek *eidos*, shape or form). Experience without thought is obviously empty and utterly meaningless ('too little comprehended'), since meaning is given by thought. The events become 'symbolic', then are distilled to their higher meaning, as 'eidolons'. But these can be seen directly in the sea and the winds, in the workings of nature.
   The passage gives examples of particular objects and realities, which then become 'such images' of meaning, the touchstones of recurrent beauty. There can be no more emotional passage in the poem than this one, and yet it is also the most intellectual:

Beauty is ordered in nature
    as the wind and sea
shape each other for pleasure; as the just
know, who learn of happiness
    from the report of their own actions.

More particularly, what I discovered in writing *Europe* was the great wave of emotion, the cumulative energy of a sea-like rhythm, that gathers in a long poem. I discovered that a long poem, in this case a series of poems, achieves an intensity and a self-propelling force that can never be equalled by short poems or a mere collection of short poems written at different times. I discovered that poetry has actual momentum, that it is like a tide, or like the sea.

※ ※ ※

    This is *Europe*, then. The sources of some of its rhythms, in Whitman, in Homer, in Jeffers, in Edgar Lee Masters, Aldington, Sandburg, Williams or Pound, are absorbed in the actual rhythms of the sea, a fact which I could vouch for when I went on a second ocean voyage to Europe, many years later, and feeling the rhythm of those waves, began to remember and almost to parody the rhythms of that poem. For the sea-waves were there in the first place, as Pound says of the birds which were there in the trees, before the 'Canzone degli uccelli' (Song of the Birds) in his 75th Canto had been written. And as the Sea at Paumanok was there before Whitman ever began to hear it.

    My relation to Pound, by the way, has often been misread and misapplied. 'Pound cake' is what A.J.M. Smith called this poem; and 'a domestic E.P.' what one of the Origin poets tried to do me in with for good. There must be a reason for such asperities, resentments, literary murders: something that gets under the skin, in the nature of the poetry, that accounts for the irritation. In other words, a new poetry, a vibration of its own kind, provokes antagonism from people who have defined tastes (or prejudices). Actually, a moment's thought will show that there is no resemblance between Ezra Pound, as man or poet, and myself – we were entirely different in sensibility, personality, aesthetic, mental process, feeling. If I quote him, or parody him, I do not necessarily resemble him.

This hardly needs to be said. We admire something that has the qualities we value, in ourselves and in the world. As we are 'influenced', our own uniqueness comes to embody these qualities ('the real I myself', as Whitman says in that poem of Eidolons). But we had them first, as the desired ideal out there, as Plato explains so well.

I should only remark in closing that the Copyright line and the 'Note' in the original book now puzzle me, and only make sense when I realize how light-hearted I was – we were – when these poems were written and first published. 'Officina Poetarum et Pictorum' is a fancy name for 'Poets' and Painters' Press' in London, who printed the book. 'Officina' comes from Pound's Canto 1: 'In officina Wecheli, 1538, out of Homer.' The fake imprint 'Laokoön Press' – really Contact Press – refers to Lessing's *Laokoön* and also to Irving Babbitt's book *The New Laokoön*, of which I once possessed a treasured copy. (This footnote could lead to a complete essay, but I must refrain.) And '... if we want a place in utopia,' now makes me think of Atlantis, the never-realized ideal world, to which all reality must somehow be referred.

'Inaccuracy'? There are probably many inaccuracies. I have corrected a few. They are nothing to boast about. Also, a few judicious cuts (nothing that would be missed).

It is the text of the poem that has now been much improved. I have always been disappointed with the printed text of the original book, because I had neglected in the proofreading to insist on having the book largely reset and made to conform to my exact layout of the poems, particularly as to the indentation of the lines. Some return to the shape of the original manuscript was made in the extracts in my *Collected Poetry* (1971). But this edition brings the entire poem back to its true form. A great satisfaction, because arrangement on the page is part of the aesthetic of poetry; and the technique of indentation in this poem, which is a delicate modulation of voice and meaning, was the beginning of a development which has continued in my poetry to the present. There are some readers, I hope, who will be interested in these things, who do not read simply, or merely, for what the poem says, which is important, but is only one part of the mystery.

Louis Dudek

I. *Sea and Land*

I

Cleaving out through the clean St. Lawrence,
cellophane sweeps crisp with contemporaneity,
the shores receding ...
          going out to sea ...

          Bridge
parties in the lounge,
      and tourist chatter:

Time's newest, flimsiest, cheapest crinkles
      unwrapping Vacation Tours –
'Let's finish this hand'
      'I've had enough'

Travelling tourist class, to Europe
      out of American, Canadian cities.

What are we going to find?
      What are we going to see?

2

This is not yet the sea, it is the river.
For a long time we have been
only on the river, the rocking-horse waves
of a minor reality, Newton's invention:
roof slates on a mechanical surface,
dollar bills of green, small froth of holiday beer
          and ice-cream soda.

The river between green banks
holds in the mocked tide
beyond Quebec, beyond Megantic, Restigouche.
Dotted with Donald Duck villages
the shore mounts like a flapjack
on either side. Bridged here and there by cantilevers,
scooped by the dredger, man.

Nowhere is it so noisy, nowhere so unnatural & noisome
as (singing some yoo-ooo love song)
here on this river; yet it is the realest thing,
your present, a gift of time,
the tamed moment of eternity
                 for you,
flowing on and out into the sea, where we go.

3

Even on a river you will find great puddles of froth
                trying to beat up a sea.
Even in June an occasional ice-floe (was it?)
                or a sea-gull's wing.

A river tears down its banks and graves its deepest ruts
as deep as it can, bores away, chasm to peneplain
before it gives way and gives in.
                A river is a member of the sea;
of sky-sperm, sky fathered, flowing down free
                to its blood-purple parent.

4

The biggest waves in this water
are those we make ourselves.

But why fish
in someone else's backwash?

There was a time when I was satisfied
with fishing in the clean St. Lawrence,
the Little Jesus River
        (no sooner Souster heard it
                but he put it in a poem),
whiskered bullheads, sweet slim perches,
soup fish in summer.
'Ça mord-t-il?' we used to shout
        to the fishermen under the bridge.

A plodding sport, for the trivial imagination,
              of waiting, waiting –
then it comes, a small civilized
              fish
that dies practically in your hand.

Can you live – or die – for such pleasure?
If you have grown to manhood
        and strong reaching desire?

Yet there are people
who want no other art, or life
        (though there's no profit in it)
– weekends little better than a long sleep,
      or walking in sleep.
Like Bob, who made it a point of pride
to catch a five-pound pike in any water!

How to lure out the last sleeping whopper
      out of a pond – yes, there's 'art' in that.
But where we go, there are no shores.

5

Quebec lives by the river, by the slim St. Lawrence.
But for the river, Champlain
would not have found it,
Cartier would not have gone so far,
nor La Salle settled. The ocean liner
comes here and takes us out,
takes wheat, silver, paper;
and the fish come here,
fresh fish, that taste best salted, the sea fish,
the sea salmon, that dies in the mountains.

The river made these cities. Last night
the Chateau and its brood of houses
stood for a moment in soft pastel colours
        on the sky as we passed;
then the lights beyond it a *via lactea*,
stretching for miles beyond, and Lévis,
both in the mouth of the St. Lawrence,
shone – the river buttons; the rest, night
        cloaking a cold continent.

Three Rivers is named for it, and raids on the land
as well as on the ocean, stripping forests.
                              Montreal
raids on the world for population,
Hungarians, Poles, Mongolians, Greeks and Jews,
as well as the two conventional races
who stiffen against each other in their pride.
        Too much to lose!

The river brings them its mixed blessings,
other people's broken wrongs; brought its
accumulation of dead habits,
the racial tics of other nations.
Prisoners, castaways, the poor, the malcontents
              came to the colonies.
Raw matter for a raw country,
too often wasted and withered there, unused, left to dry.

6

What the river made, it has also unmade,
having too little power
to break down differences,
to force by violence
and make us love.
The river here has been too gentle and too kind
and we have taken its cold comfort
without winning by right
fighting the elements, or men.
The river has told us, everything
you need will now be yours
(though others earned it)
only you must be sensible
and, as I am, confined.

7

The merest survival is all that most of
mankind is concerned with
(on this ship, simple but substantial
Dutch cooking) –
what they relish beyond that, however,
is what makes them beautiful or hateful.

8

The Indians would have been surprised.
A canoe is all right,
    or a sail on the water
(Won't disturb the ducks –
    just another mortal enemy).
But this
    Evil of whirling knives
making mincemeat of the water,
    with what they call 'electricity',
spoiling the atmosphere
    all the way to Dover:
this is devil, is contrary to GREAT SPIRIT
    – if a ship can be that important.
It will come to no good.

No, they would not have liked the big mumbo-jumbo
    of this magic.

9

Land is delightful, whatever islands,
St. Pierre & Miquelon,
whatever mountains
we pass, are delightful and habitable places
we look at wondering
      how it would be there
to fish there, hunt, set up houses,
whether cities will spring up someday
      in the Shickshocks,
           in tracts of Newfoundland,
already, see, there are people
           there, there
St. Pierre & Miquelon, fishing islands
      (French still, 1660/1814, taken, ceded)
the last we shall see,
      and then the sea....

10

But I had not known the sea would be this splendid
                magnificent lady:
'destroyer of ships, of cities'
in luxurious ermine and leopard coat
                sighing in the ship's wake;

destroyer of civilizations, of pantheons,
to whom Greece and Rome are only a row of white breakers
spilled with a hush, in air,
then marbled patterns on a smoother wave ...

And I would not be surprised if the sea made Time
in which to build and to destroy
as it builds these waves and indolently breaks them,
                or if the whole fiction
of living were only a coil in her curvature
                of immense imagination.

Maker and breaker of nations, sea of resources,
you have enough here for a million rivers,
                for a billion cities,
enough for new Judaea, for new Alexandria,
and Paris once again, and America's morning.

11

New men and new women!
         – The sea is so easily bored!
And treacherous ... in love ...
              like any woman.
Beware, O nations, of her coiled and serpentine body.

12

Here the dead are very familiar,
Davy Jones and all his fellows,
those who walked the plank and died in storms
or plummeted down in silent coffins.
The sea has swallowed so many
(and what is land if not a crust of its selvage,
earth swallowing its dead, doing the sea's business ...)
The dead become very familiar,
Shelley, Edward King,
                commemorated,
those athletes on the Titanic,
                all the Olympians, of Salamis, Trafalgàr –
familiar. And to the victor
a crown of white foam and these cheers
over and over again.

13

And the sea is a conqueror so strong it likes to be slashed for pleasure
by any new ship cleaving its waves,
it likes to be slit and slashed, splashed and splayed,
that white steeples and towers may rise
      on its recurrent crowns,
tickle the folds of its green mantle,
ruffle the hair of its infinite curling locks.

14

Columbus with all kinds of cockeyed notions
just had to keep on going and he was sure to find it,
the alchemists with all kinds of cockeyed notions ...
Explore the sea for any reason,
   and you are bound to come upon treasure.
Keep active, persist in folly,
just keep on going,
   keep mixing, even with your hands.
The sea has everything, it's the globed universal belly
   bulging with wombs.

15

And now it seems that the biggest waves
are those that come to our ship.
We can make nothing of that.
The shapeless water, an amoebic monster,
    expands and contracts around us, undecided
whether to swallow or extrude
    this shaped object of petrified foam.
So we play deck tennis, shuffleboard,
we lie wrapped in blankets,
we laugh, and make each other laugh
on our jolly excursion;
        but the sea
begins to torture our bowels
as if it would make us understand:
    possibly without design,
its influence makes itself known
by an internal shudder,
its great spasms contract our little stomachs
and in the midst of glee
    we become suddenly sick.

16

The sea loves to move
        but it is in no hurry,
flops over languidly like an easy animal
waiting for storms,
            never still.

17

'Just a lot of water,' someone says.
But when the seas begin to dry
the earth itself will become parched
                    and bare as the moon.

This water contains its living animals
and all the living animals the world contains
come from this water ...

All that is good in us is still whatever of the sea
                    we contain.

18

Let your body
move with the rhythm of the ocean,
you can learn to suffer
recorded cacophony, conversation, or cards
clogging the belly,
if you yield to her magnificent surges
that divide like logs
under each explosion of surf
and settle
like earth after underground dynamite
has swelled it.

O let your body
rise and fall to this new river
the sea bears
trailing from old Quebec to older
nobler cities,
learn to be borne
gladly on its unexhausted waves
and be made new, if she is willing.

19

The commotion of these waves, however strong, cannot disturb
                      the compass-line of the horizon
nor the plumb-line of gravity, because this cross coordinates
                      the tragic pulls of necessity
that chart the ideal endings, for waves, and storms
                      and sunset winds:
the dead scattered on the stage in the fifth act
– Cordelia in Lear's arms, Ophelia, Juliet, all silent –
show nature restored to order and just measure.
                      The horizon is perfect,
and nothing can be stricter
than gravity; in relation to these
                      the stage is rocked and tossed,
kings fall with their crowns, poets sink with their laurels.

20

It is possible, however, that with radar and steel rings
one might conquer the ocean.
    That is our tragedy.
For us, the thing has no more fear,
        and as you say, is a lot of water;
will be harnessed next
    for cooking or electric power.
And we can afford to be such fools, for our time.
The sea is indifferent.
A giant, wound up in strings, tied up by Lilliputians,
he seems to sleep a long while
    – perhaps waiting until we are all dead,
perhaps until we are perfectly sure we have succeeded,
and then he will heave his chest to yawn
        one morning,
and quietly drown the continents,
      just turning over in his siesta.

21

From eleven every morning the programme reads 'Concert',
but it turned out to be bebop
    exclusively and German *Sehnsucht*
of Nelson Eddy vintage.
        'How about Mozart?
            Or the *Messiah*?'
piped an American collegian.
        'Let's relax!'
The intellectual calibre (high on this voyage)
is about that of the *Sat. Eve. Post*
but as for entertainment the same
does for all 'cattle' (the trade name for passengers).
    What does the sea care
regarding the noise we make?
The sea does not care,
but it makes its meaning plain:
crossing the ocean swell to jazz rhythms
we are certainly a Ship of Fools!

The sea is the only measure of music.

22

Having boarded the ship as an innocent
I had not realized that an ocean crossing
is one of our fucking institutions,
the top deck at night is a Coney Island,
cocktails whirling in crazy currents
every night in the dancehall, a shipboard romance
is part of everybody's business,
who's making who tonight, that's the question,
we are all caught in the damned human maelstrom,
forgetting the ocean, the thing doesn't matter
except as a place to feel ourselves adrift in
in every sense, cut off from the outer,
the worlds on either side, free to go nuts with
this modern idea of pleasure
creating a temporary eight-day culture
without a chance of survival
beyond the immediate present,
a freak wave in the shilly-shallying water,
not to be repeated, certainly soon forgotten.

But I have never passed up an opportunity,
and who cares how a society gratifies
the rollicking 'free rhythms' of the umbilicus
so long as it does so, let's be conventional,
the waves around here have certainly started something,
with two hundred interesting bodies (and one or two minds)
to pick from, one ought to be satisfied: Darling,
just lay your head against my shoulder and the sea
will do the rest, sex at least can be satisfactory and simple.

23

Much of the time now we forget that we're moving on water.
There's no more need to be always aware of the sea
               than there is to be aware of the land.
It's there. It won't go away.
That's just the trouble with trying to pretend
it's not, in order to cure your small private headache.
Our stomachs are now settled.
We don't mind stumbling against each other
               in the corridors.
So even Fools are eventually
               assimilated,
there is no object so lopsided
               but it has an exact centre of gravity.
No one is rejected
from nature. That's why
               we suffer so for our mistakes.

24

Ironic? How could the sea be
        that small!
Or indifferent? Not either.
        To all this!
With lecherous slobbering lips
        everlastingly amorous
                but satisfied
she wouldn't grudge us a few crumbs
        of her own comfort.
I suppose we can thank the air
        for continually loving her up and down;
I suppose it is just another way
        she has of dragging us all in –
the cosy, self-satisfied, beastly
        madam!

25

Strange, that in the midst of all this deep-
        sea novelty and nonsense
I think of someone far away
at the end of the world
        where we started,
crossing Dominion Square from St. Antoine
or eating lunch on St. Catherine
        and looking so sad
you'd think the whole world was dying
            and this was his sister,
then she unties the tight little bow-knot
        of her mouth
and sparks out like a small red firecracker
– till you'd think it was
        the last Victoria Day –
and you know from that small bang
      how wonderfully youth has advanced ahead of us
with new explosives
        and the world-wrecking business.

26

It's a small world, a very small world
                we move in,
but it takes us by the heart,
                    takes us in
before we know it, and we hate to part with it.

The gesture was really significant,
                on new land, we thought it important
and we took pictures, of each putting his first foot on it.

Meeting and parting, the champagne
                of life goes to these occasions.

We have left our world, we have left America,
                and we are here.

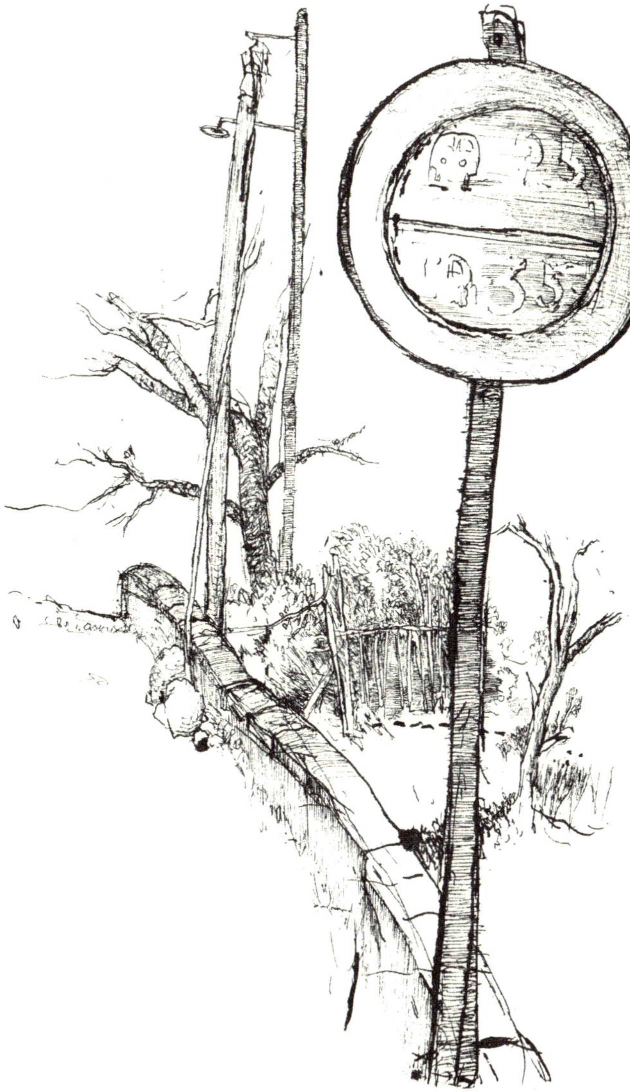

II. *England*

27

A city is a kind of ship,
most of it an old tramp
most of it salt-eaten
sea-stained, encrusted
with lives beyond recall;
some of it new
decked with modern apartments
flying flags and bunting
for life's excursion pleasures;
much of it freight and trade.

A city is a kind of ship,
it touches the ports of time –
Past and Present – the wharves of space
– Here and Now – it comes and goes
making its long voyage
and then sinks in the sand:
Troy, Ecbatan, buried cities.

28 *Southampton*

Ruins are beautiful,
    the city was half demolished
            by bombs
At first we did not understand
why all the signs of demolition, stumps
    of houses, overgrown with grass.

Ugly city, we said,
if you had the choice of living
    here or living all your life on shipboard
it would be hard to choose which
    would be less uncomfortable –
nor that both don't have their points.
The horticultural side of England,
        tiny gardens
before the dingiest of houses,
    roses and exotic silly trees,
quaint, at once, let's hope for all
And that class deference
    which puts you in your place, up or down,
        once for all
But for the most part, the sordid and depressing habits
    of the poor, accustomed to be poor.

A city of wharves sloppy with the sea,
            Southampton
City of old decrepitude and new vulgarity
Ugly city, I said
until I saw the ruined churches, weeds growing
    on the broken walls
and understood the demolitions.

Ruins are beautiful
We will see some more glorious, more renowned
                        than these
But the ugly, like the strong, who have suffered
                        are beautiful,
And bombs have done this much for contemporaneity.
I think of the black eggs falling
                        out of the sky
and their furious spawn
                        (we bought a leather hand-grip
from a dealer bombed out of the corner block
                        he once had)
And it is pleasant to see how right and decent
                        after all, this town is –
more real, and in the present, because death has touched it.

29

I guess nature, uncultivated, precedes us
not without form,
        but the Sussex downs
have had two thousand years of it –
English culture. Even the fields could not remain
        uncivilized
after that. Nature
is lovely here, a garden, in England.
The shape one gives the land
        is conventional:
a sentimental culture
    like the English whose secret, common sense,
leaves no room for reality
        of imagination
makes even nature cosy, the oaks parks,
a landscape weeping like a watery Turner.

30

There was a ship's lock on Russell's door,
the literary place
            of England.
We talked about Pound and bragged.
        The ship rocked
as the beer foamed. In England
no conversation can be pursued
                beyond the first offence.
So we went to bed.

The reality of any country, as the tourist learns
is in the art it has made.
           The rest, which seems so real,
is ships of paper, will drown.

We planned for the future,
books and things, Niemojowski
                  had three projects.
All this counts, though nobody heard
how we launched paper battleships.
                  Anyhow,
look at the thing from both sides, power
seems to matter, but doesn't matter at all
          in the long run,
and what the few make, almost in secret,
may go on for centuries.

31

The ignorant present has scribbled over the past
                                  at Winchester;
an American goon
painted on the door
      saying 'yak yak' to all this
rectangular proud English Gothic.

At first there was nothing, the beginning
was hardest, then what they made
      was made out of what they had begun.
No matter. The present is shaped out of the first
      shaped stones,
                    from Stonehenge to this.

It is all flowers within
      and fluted stems,
'Music,' you said, and 'One cannot believe
it is of stone,' such intricate
      articulations
of white bone, and terrible black
                mediaeval magic.

But there is nothing,
      nothing in the nineteenth century additions:
the recent cemetery sculpture
beside the older, sombre, Norman Gothic
that did not try to be beautiful.
                        Only true.

To what? Consider for instance
        the harrowing tomb of Richard Fox
showing his body
     lacerated by suffering and death,
there to tell you
– do not be too gay, even if God
        doesn't particularly matter,
the bones remain, they are the cathedral.

But several tourists
       have scrawled their names
on the breast of Richard Fox
     just where the skeleton comes through the skin.
Let these additions remain
         in Winchester
Perhaps time will prove
such fools, like sculptured animals
belong here after all.
     They would have had no stone
to write so plainly on, if death had not offered them
          its bony breast.

London, this is not what I have come to see.
This is the present, I have seen it
               in New York, in Toronto,
the same crowds at lunch time, the same lunch counters,
                   banks, and shopping centres.
People, without a place, without a time but the moment,
rags in the hungry wind that tears them to pieces:
the fictive storm-at-sea, without order, without calm.

33

Courtesy is pleasing, saves us from barbarism.
In London, a frozen whirlpool of purple water,
courtesy is the memory of whispered spray
and gentleness that once smoothed the waters.

One sees the kings in wax, the Lords' seats
in Westminster, the fashionable cathedral
built by Wren, and the squares where Addison's
feet may have stepped; Gainsborough at the Tate;

sentiment and vacuity in English art, blame it
on the eighteenth century, blame it on respectability.
What is left of it, in crowded Trafalgar Square
& by bombed banks in Fleet Street, is a kind of softness

in a dying culture, saving the last good thing
before the onslaughts of unconformity come
and free unreason. But kindness is very welcome.
And what more pleasant than well-bred English people?

34 *Covent Garden*

What the head of the schoolboy heard
who held his ear against the prima donna's breast
all the time that she sang her aria:
the source of all music,
      a noise in the shelled heart of a woman.
She flung her notes against the prows of druid rocks
and they echoed back to us.
          For time is a great wall
to carry echoes, whatever we see or hear.
This is London. Tonight
there are two musics – in Covent Garden
and in Whitehall, the auditorium of power.
But to hear the first sound, where they are one,
that would be more than music.

35

The black excrement of the factories,
Birmingham, Manchester
              for miles and miles
smears over the country,
so dismal we must hide our eyes
from rows of silent buildings, old rust, new grime.
If ever they leave ruins
        black crickets only will sing their praise.
What is England? The beautiful gardens
        of Sussex, the Lakes,
are not her empire, her power;
it is this monstrous dream
we have tried to traverse quickly, at night,
        which still haunts our morning
with brick, with smokestacks,
        the nightmare reality we cannot shake,
which is her victory, the dark angel
        of our world.

36 *Lancaster*

Here you can sit and understand
how one building can civilize a city,
     and the stalls of the Priory
hoary but always new
   (like Shakespeare's every word,
   good as when it was written)
make them rugged but kind.
They have built even their stables and garages
of that stone, and the streets are all architecture.
Old England is in this corner.
And I prefer it to Oxford.
    It is more common, still unpossessed
by those who would use beauty
      for an advantage.
There is such a thing as being over-civilized.
   But one building
is enough, where people are receptive and somewhat rude.

37

Wordsworth certainly picked it, the best part of England
        for the sort of thing he wanted.
I had not thought it would be this
                sensational.
The rest of England is quiet countryside, flat to the east,
        rolling hills southward;
Cornwall and Wales have mountains, but here
        the surprises make one laugh –
a parody of romantic scenery, now highly cultivated
        and trimmed like the French poodle
with rock fences, hedges. Holiday travel
        has put a premium on the town houses,
motor coaches stream in and out of the steep hills, crowded
        with nature lovers.
Here you see what a poet can do to real estate:
        though that was clear to be seen at Stratford.
Wordsworth has outdone Shakespeare, by making his poems
        as sizeable and safe as these mountains.
What's why the English love him. Though I doubt
whether many today who holiday here
        think much in passing of his name.

38 *York, Lincoln, Peterborough, Ely*

Judging from these buildings, the English were once a people
who were not the least in such things –
                           the visceral expression
of artistic vigour, to the point of religion.
The English are now a Milquetoast nation
      constrained by a tailored straitjacket
of what is or is not done. They call this their virtue,
            but it is deadly
to all that making buildings like these demands.
Art, or 'beauty', cannot be cultivated
      as you, ladies and gentlemen, would approve.
Look at the beastly gargoyles,
                  look up at these pinnacles,
they will teach you again how to feel.
Paradise is such a place;
        it stands over Inferno
and would be cold, but for its central heating.

39

A momentary disturbance, which looked like a fatal accident
                at embarkation,
at Dover, the grey cliffs, reminding us
that all we see for our pleasure has tragic features;
as London had, Birmingham,
nine-tenths of every ancient city
      hauling, grinding, and smelting
                        the human flesh –
the horror, in short, of contemporary living.
The man hurt, walked limping away after.

Overlooking Dover the castle stands,
              a landmark for the tourist trade.
(They say Hitler promised himself a dinner
      over there; an old-fashioned idea,
                      like any war.)

To the new England, old ruins
      are unimportant, of sentimental value.
The power of machinery is very great. But the imagination
that shapes machinery has nothing to do with ruins
or with the lovely countryside: the enigma
of our tortured lives cannot be answered
                        by visiting an island.
Yet there is a perfect harmony, looked at from the water,
in the cliffs, the castle, and the industrial city under them.
The strong black line at sea level,
            the castle almost in clouds,
and the white and green cliffs rising to meet them.

40

There is something disturbing in being again on water,
        I ask the white sea
if there is life anywhere
as foaming, as glowing green, as this;
        if land can possibly be, or have,
ever, all that the sea contains.
Monuments fool us, delude us into believing
        that once there was energy
married with equity, to raise such buildings.
But there also was pride and oppressive power,
there also (a dungeon, stocks and irons) they built for killing.
The commonplace and the brutish, serf and master
and proud priest; rotting straw on thatched roofs,
slit homestead walls of an ancient farm –
this dirt of the past may as well be cleaned out.
Why should we ride into eight hundred years ago
        to see others as foul as ourselves?
If now only the proud cathedrals remain,
                it is because art
outlives inhumanity.

History is really the study of failures,
                the best buildings
lack some points of proportion, dimension.
Only the sea makes her circle perfect.

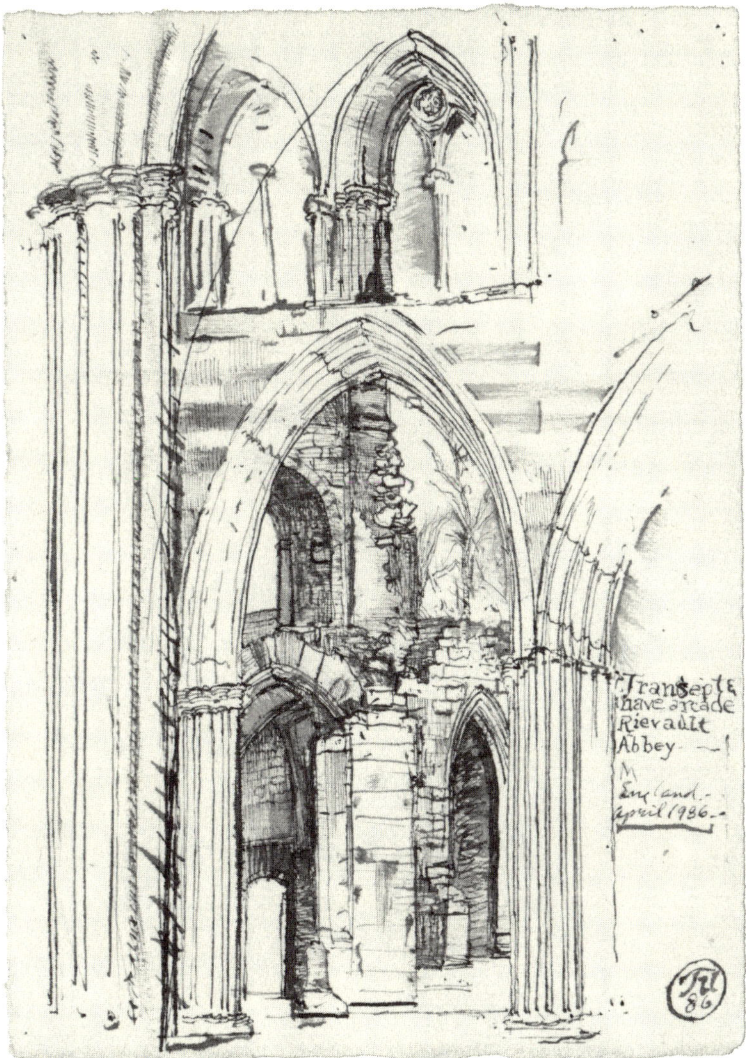
Transepts &
nave arcade
Rievault
Abbey
England
April 1986

III. *France*

41

Across the level fields of France
extensive as empire or continent
        the wind over the wheat
runs in delicate timid waves, moonlit in daytime.

They cultivate every acre
        with geometrical exactitude
as they built their cathedrals with grace.
        We found this true.

The beautiful mind of the cultivated Frenchman
        must be like these fields, these waves,
an undulation measured like the dance
        of Cleopatra's body.

42

I suppose that what you see
depends on who you are.
                  A busload of tourists
stopped by the cathedral of Amiens without looking
        at it at all, went in for coffee or to piss,
not one stood in the blazing sunlight looking upward.
                    When they rode away
we were left in the dust they raised, our eyes itching
                from that savage crystal,
with the great round window in the dark waiting.

43

On the roads to Paris, truckdrivers urinate
quite naturally on the this-side of trees.
One learns easily. That is the difference
between England and the French. Not an advantage
exactly to either side. Bidets in hotel rooms,
the street urinals of Paris, simply disgusting
to any aesthetic sense. Why on earth
    parade all your functions in public
just because you're that human? Even farting
can be done amicably, among a few; but with two million
people to accommodate, is it any wonder
        that standards vanish?

44

Parisian intellectuals I think would laugh
at that performance of Shakespeare in Stratford.
It was nevertheless the finest we had ever seen.
So much the right thing, of course, which is the best
part of England. Paris is neither here nor there.
A city of liars and thieves, in the first place.
They amuse themselves, true, but it is nature
expressed in a special set of habits, Parisian pleasures,
and only the French way will do. Suppose you don't like it?
'The worst chauvinists in the world,' says Logue.
Nobody has any work to do, or responsibility;
and they consider this really living, either as artists
or café intellectuals. Where does the money
come from? Home. The tourists. They live on nothing:
even the income from poems can keep them going.
Living in a lovely cottage on the downs
in England is no better solution. One wants an occupation
that serves the world, not for cash but for the sake of the work.
And that isn't easy to find, all occupations are now against it.

45

Love at all corners and songs
            all night, all day
Yes, Paris is gay, as they say, nobody works
     everybody loves, whatever they do they do enjoy.
All morning the fruitstalls and markets stand open,
        at 13 o'clock they close,
the little family sets up table
     in the place of affairs, takes bread and wine.
To sell they refuse, and it's impolite to disturb.
The waiters in the cafés try not to serve,
     you drink what you can get,
              just sit and enjoy ...
They say in the world there is despair,
    la crise, le désarroi (Gide and his boys,
             and Sartre somewhere in the caves)
But the Parisians are gay, a city of clowns,
and though there's no special meaning to it all
        – it's gay!

When you return home in Paris
                    at 24 o'clock
all the lovers in the street make way for you
as you ride, as they walk
                along the street;
they open before you like a midnight flower
composed of lovers, every petal two
                and in the middle of the flower,
                                – you.

47

In the Place de la Concorde, where the guillotine stood
                and did so much good
and did so much harm, we walked arm in arm
and got lost in the Louvre
            that royal museum
with all those great bargains in art-books and cards.
King Louis in marble stood by then and smiled
            at how we presumed
to look unimpressed by the size of his rooms
              (so different the Renault from his coach-and-six,
different the traffic from tumbrils and sticks),
              but in the Place
de la Concorde six days later
the familiar tables were turned
            once more, & a broken bottle hissed
as the bullets shot by the police
              hit or missed.
All to demonstrate ... what?... (King Louis smiles)
– that there is still no peace, but a sword,
            in the Place de la Concorde.

48

Paris, more stinking royal than any city:
    city of republicans, of the Conciergerie, Bastille!
(Some 10,000 visit Versailles on a Sunday?
    Nothing but sentiment. O the great age
    of the Roi Soleil!)
The city is filled with palaces and baroque horrors
and such filthy flamboyant statues
    as deface the corners of the best cathedrals,
    even Chartres –
eighteenth-century additions, twentieth-century
    legs et dons.
And buried under Paris, under the Palais de Justice,
    under St. Germain & the Louvre,
you will find the stained glass
    of the Sainte Chapelle,
and a small Greek church of very early date,
and St. Séverin, perfect and harmonious, and quiet,
and the staring face of Notre Dame.

49

Only in Chartres, under the dome
    (two towers, and three windows
    such as God had not seen before)
and the Virgin everywhere, and in the centre
    looking into the nave
streaming with colour so that you almost weep,
    so that you sit
for half an hour in one place, under the dome,
    looking four ways,
under the dome of Chartres
    (about which I cannot speak,
    have really no right to talk)
I knew in the very centre what had gone wrong
    in Paris, and understood Versailles.
'How could they give up this?'
'Entertainment, amusement, have eaten up the arts!'
And fossil French classicism, which France cannot outlive.
Exhibitions of the rich, debasing ancient art
    for female self-adornment and display –
like the phylloxera, have eaten at the root.
For which they have abandoned Chartres.

50

The Greeks were fine, but French classicism
using the Greek for its own purpose,
smooth hypocrisy, conceit, & the display
                of that corruption, *le bon goût,*
– the worst taste in manners or in art
                the world has ever seen –
spoiled two centuries of European art,
opened the arts to worse corruption still –
                the monstrous sugar teeth
of 'money' and 'amusement': here you see
                        in Chartres
art is no entertainment, it does not amuse;
money paid for it, but it paid for
                something that the sculptor really preferred;
pride was satisfied, but it was pride
                in objects, the full scale
of human performance – they worked for this, gladly.
The wedge of ignorance entered Europe
                with a blind idolatry
of Greece and Rome; you can see it
          as a straight line from the fifteenth century down,
'art for art', copying the Greek forms,
shape without sense, imitating
                imitations, dramatic motion, sensuality
for the boudoir, decorativeness
to make room for gold, for size.

After this, there was no honesty
whether in art or trade, to fight off the incisor
of the pure profiteer, the hog
with his snout in the mire, his belly in shit.
The Gothic tower had fallen,
                the last craftsman
dropped his hammer; it has come
to all of us, poets, advertisers,
dance hall singers and all,
we make our pilgrimage to Chartres, without praying beads;
look at the Virgin helpless, and up to the great dome
        where the light seems to rise and fall.

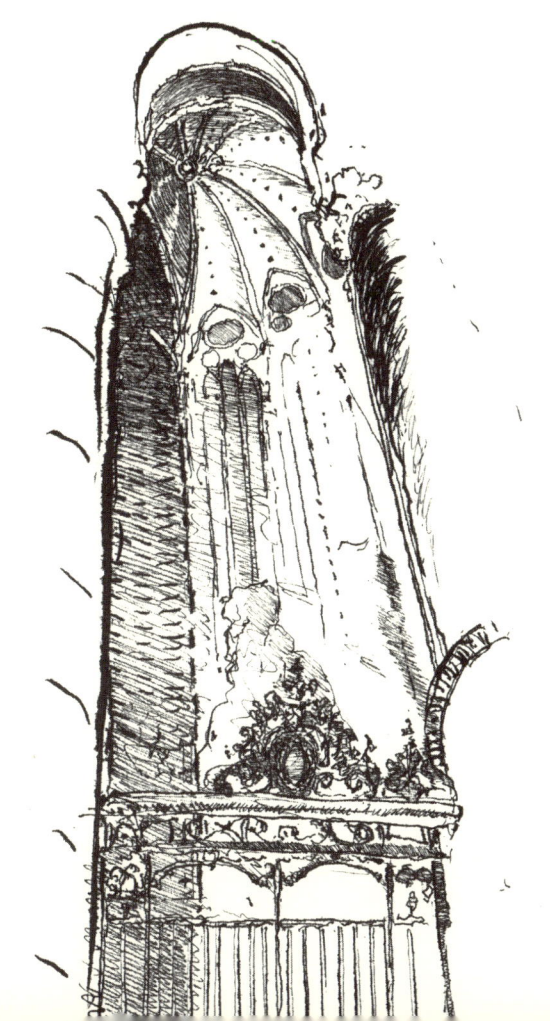

51

The French, as to intellect, are nothing
very exceptional, i.e., the common
man, *la classe ouvrière*, very pleasant, illiterate
as everywhere, the difference
is in their very marked character, habits
going back for centuries no doubt, such as
inaudible syllables, shrugs and gestures,
the closing of shops at uncustomary hours –
'to hell with business' – the head-dress at Chartres,
however, was really affected, for purposes of selling
hand-made mittens (you bought a pair),
and of course the habit
of wines and bidets, since nature,
said Pascal, is the first habit; but as to intellect
it comes to very little; and where, one might ask
does even that come from? An exceptional
individual, as in America? A concealed
aristocracy, not in these towns and villages?
The only part of intellect worth attending
is the local and popular, what you see
in the market, the streets – Utrillo
had it all handed to him, Cocteau
no doubt in the cafés learned it,
brilliant in consequence, a way of talking.
So these people are really artists, like the chambermaid
who talked a musical score, in Paris,
like the boy who danced on a bicycle.
'A city of clowns'; but a clown
is a poet in action, says Henry Miller.
Only in the country, is it depressing
to see the clowns-out-of-work, the sad
panorama of a deserted circus.
France, like any modern nation,
keeps all its valuables in one city.

52

After the thirteenth century it all deteriorates.
Three centuries
        of show-off excesses
and smooth shellacking introduce the baroque.
They discovered the Gothic
        prayerful arches
at first flat and ascetic
        as at Chartres, the façade
and the plain tower;
then to glorify the Virgin, or Christ
        or the city (it may be) that made it,
flamboyant, glittering with jewels,
        fluting and fanning upward,
            splitting up the light with colours.
This was Gothic: expelling evil spirits
        out of the gables,
e.g., a cat on the corner, turning his head toward you,
        or animals eating each other.
By the seventeenth century, the smoothies
        had learned how to cut an arch
or a cornice with the brainless exactitude
        of precision instruments,
and made them all alike: one sees it
        in the chapel at Amboise
where Leonardo's body lies, though part of the doorway,
the carving, is true, in the old style,
the rest is repetition, pattern without significance,
        animals no longer endearing
            or brutal
simpering virgins in contemporary dress –
        French, as Europe has known it
for these 300 years of French pseudo-culture.

Look at the French
>   Renaissance and the eighteenth century,
look at 'toilet tile gothic'
and nineteenth-century *gloire, empire* –
>   'classicism.'
But they are not to blame;
>   we have come into disgusting centuries
where everything grows worse perpetually,
the sewage floating on the tide
>   where the white wave was broken.
And only now
only now we begin to see, begin with despising
all that bad taste
and monarchic idiocy, that corruption
in man and society through 500 years;
only now, looking for one or two
>   objects or men, in all Europe,
the few who work from the centre
wrestling with the evil before them
>   in what they say, making the words
ring true to nature –
we seem to turn on the foetid tide
>   of history,
making for clean water.

Not Catholic, but universal,
>   this vision,
no existentialist betrayal
>   of Pericles or Copernicus:
to carve the line
>   positive and true
in the smallest detail, and in the large
harmonious with the body;
to follow the rise and fall of the greater tide.

53

Under the rocks at Biarritz
where the sea rushes in, in terraces
                of white breakers
toward the tourists scattered on the crisp spattered sand –
the two protagonists of this epos,
                the latter creating
hotel fronts
& zebra umbrellas
as usual;
the sea carving the architraves of the ragged rocks.

Beauty is a form of energy.

When that is depleted, pleasure
            or comfort, is all that the organism desires.
The apparent energy of the factories
           and industrial sites, so ugly,
        which we have seen in France and in England
              (the length and breadth of them)
is really exhaustion, not power, so far as the worker
        is concerned, in his dismal dwellings;
despair because there is no beauty.
And the masters of that system, whom we can now see, if we want to,
            will be brutal beings, desperate
in their ignorant search for enjoyment and power;
they cannot be dedicated
or happy in the expression
           of their virility,
nor feel in their veins the sea as they work.

Hence the rich are great drinkers
of hard liquor, and come to these resorts
wearing short trousers,
having shaved their legs cleanly,
their arms like coffee. They sit confidently
in deck chairs, or under tents
listening to the tame ocean,
while all Europe is a heap of ruins
covered over with new buildings; new voices
        fill the air where the hammer
chipped the rock once, the bell tolled
serenely. We take the spray on our faces
        like tiny tears
from that great duct which is green and golden.
Can you hear?
The sea is angry, because they have deceived her
        and lied to her.

54

A Hendaye les enfants
   jouent dans la mer, les enfants
joyeux comme la mer joyeuse;
leurs formes minces dans les vagues dansantes
dansent comme des lumières
à travers de vieux vitraux:
   rouges chemises, et corps
      de petits saints courbés,
assis sur des roches, assis sur le mur
   qui tient l'océan en frein –
voici l'art nouveau des malheureux
      de ces temps de malheur,
danse de la joie, et de la souffrance
         libérée,
l'armée des justes qui lutte contre l'erreur.

IV. *The Warm South*

55

Yes, you should come south, to the warm south,
                      from which all Europe is visible:
San Juan de Luz, Pamplona
           (the tops of Spain),
mountains, from which all Europe is plain;
the German middle
in her intestines,
          and there, the cerebral madness
of the new life in Russia, where men are implored
to love the proletariat,
         my darling.
In France the deserted villages,
and in England no villages at all.
Look closely
         and you will see
the morning smoke of the big cities,
so unpleasant to enter,
       so good to leave behind
(they have everything
that modern man desires, especially
        shopping centres, depots, hoards of news);
you will see them empty of vision,
and the despair of *tous les jeunes,*
some turning to God, some to post-Kantian ethics,
Libérez chalked on the walls –
but not for these inhabitants
whose despair itself may be hopeful, if they will come and see
someday, how dirty their life was
                 (the young, the hostellers)
and watch the children play in the sand
      and wade here in the water.

What they will do then, nobody knows;
it may be something simple
            like building Chartres,
                        or laying down a stone.

O yes, you should come south
to see the sun rise over Pamplona
                for the fiesta,
and see the sky brighten
            and hear the cock crow in the Pyrenees.

56

To this majestic country of very simple people
the best of any art
would be an imitation
        or a bit too good to be true.
White buildings blocked out cleanly,
    and generous windows in that frame;
a red scarf, a red handkerchief,
that is as much art
    as anyone can stand. Enough!
Who would want to create beauty
where the mountains rise almost perpendicularly
        and bow in a huge landscape
of domes and arches? Why write
the grand reflective poem, or the epic,
when songs and castanets
        are as good a music?
Food is cheap and simple – fish, cheese, bread –
    and work in the fields, on the farms.
Though Franco has done much in the way of electrification
        and small industries are abounding,
the people are country people,
childlike and generous,
    whether in the city or outside.
But we come here cerebrating,
wrangling, with all our novel western habits,
washing continually, paying cash for everything,
        demanding clean accommodation.

Who are we to have opinion, we who have gambled everything
            in the Grand Casino of time?
Are we any surer of winning,
we, who are the newest, richest of history's playboys,
than the oldest common people
            who haven't a chip to throw –
yet still can command such respect?

57

Except for the bullfights,
        if you remember
how with an immense whelp of blood the *toro* fell.
Hollywood never showed this.
                And as to why,
'It's very simple,' Stephanie observed,
as she did of la Sainte Chapelle.
And so it is, the one and the other;
only why be so bloody about killing a beast?
Civilized life, we know, is a ritual,
        some of it more interesting, some less;
but why the Spaniards, who are so fine in everything,
                and innocent,
should have such hell in their bodies (as all their art
        betrays) – 'mon petit' could not explain.
All Spain smells of blood
        since that day. ('San Fermin!')

And a cross of wood stood higher than the wall
and looked into the blood-smeared arena.

58

It seems to have been the discovery of our time
that the desert is a human condition; even where it is real,
it is a loneliness within,
    not the red, or white-hot rocks that suffer.

From Pamplona to Tarragona,
    Stationes en el desierto,
where not even the grasshopper will linger.
Imagine a slab of Dakota, where it is scorchiest and gulchiest;
yet everywhere, there are terraces
    where someone tried to cultivate it,
remains of farm buildings,
signs of ploughing;
even, on the side of the mountain, there, a ploughman,
incredible spectacle, amid the rock and waste.

This is perhaps a measure
    of how hard it can get to be
        how far from water.
Strange, that it should come to us
in Spain, where we would hardly expect it: this land
brings together violent extremes.
    Tomorrow we will swim and loll in the ocean
at Tarragona, by the blue Mediterranean.

59

Where the sea smashes
      on the rocks at Bordighera:
simply for pleasure,
        like the surf at Sete,
            alone, for miles and miles
          of wind and sea-washed
                    sand

a strip of land, where there is water on both sides
and a good road running by the sea –
lonely, we stopped and stripped
for the sweet salt surf, the sea
      that took us in as though we were nothing
            (making that poem)

or on the glittering Riviera
        (hard pebbles, but good water)
where there are 30 miles also devoted entirely to pleasure,
we rested at any rate, one afternoon
              and slept there
(the Casino stupid and vulgar,
one could see the money
        raked in by the croupier,
and very little coming back)
or at *baccarat*, each betting against the other
        the House always collecting its dividends.
No art out of this, says Ezra,
there is no art where there is theft on the community
and each bets against the other.
No art in St. Raphaël,
      Nice or Cannes,

a hundred years later, 200 years later
these villas will lie in ruin
still an eyesore
    & the money and the bankers
                            no more
(says, or might say, Ezra);

but we enjoyed it
lying on the beach there and sleeping
after Spain, the fiesta,
after the ruins of Villafranca,
        the caves of Les Baux,
                vineyards, the grape country
of Spain and France, equally good,
        and the small towns of Provença.

Lay by the sea sleeping
with the Casino overhead,
        and the sea lapping quietly at our feet.

You will know by their arts,
                the fruits of a civilization.
Honest minds, like the Communist
we met at the plage with his family,
do a lot of good to make one confident
                        at least in the ferment
within the present; but what people have left
            or what they are now building
speaks from the heart and from the centre
                            of any community,
whether it is railroads or warehouses
        (the incomplete sentence) or villas
                        like a rotten egg-plant
that cannot last because they are not true
to nature, to man, what he must
        and what he would like to attain.

61

A woman prefers the sea;
but I have never enjoyed swimming
as on the left side of the *fiume Magra*
close to the bridge
    where the clear mountain water
runs no higher than your neck
and on a hot day the stream ripples cool and smooth
in the sun, by the cropped grass-bank
where we sat and talked,
& I wrote some lines, and Italy was there.

62

In the middle of the night they burst out singing,
like drunken men everywhere, I thought,
         and your nerves were overwrought;
but they had a guitar, & the player was no slouch,
and they loved their songs, though the wine
         had unstrung their voices;
it was this also that I had expected
     (kept us awake for an hour),
like the people of Pamplona dancing,
the art that is better than poetry
         or even the oldest ruins –
the art we dream of in the others.

63

A girl with a load of hay on her head,
    another leading a donkey ...
But slowly one comes to realize
that the Europe we have come to see,
of old art, stored antiquity
       and the beautiful customary life
              of towns and villages,
hardly exists at all;
everywhere, has given place to the new Europe,
              as in Spain
the decrepit pueblo beside the modern city:
a sort of international Americanism
which is not at all American perhaps
but the face of the new life everywhere
    (first grasped there
        where nothing stood in the way,
    except stiff colonialism
       and the unhereditary aristocracy
          of the Adamses and Lowells):
of factories, 'the new-rich Milanese',
              and commercial storefronts.
As in Genoa, never good for art,
that defeated Pisa,
        says Baedeker,
(judge the decay of the tourist intellect,
      the old guides against the new blue books –
    where do the French girls strip
        for *exhibition,* where are the night clubs:
           'What to See What to Do in Paris');

Genoa is greasy and full of business
of the kind already familiar,
   except that the old streets
are still as narrow
as when they built San Lorenzo,
and they do sell
   Pindemonte's Omero
      at half a dollar.
Though we have come here to see old Europe,
it is the new which really concerns us,
      here as in America.
The past speaks in the remaining monuments
   and a few pages
     of the dead poets,
judging the Esso empire
and the new Milanese
     without mercy.
What should we say, we few,
who know what we know,
    but for these records?
Where would we get words
    for our recriminations?

64

Our eyes are filled with arches, with marble colonnades,
                campaniles and towers;
when I close my lids I see them
        vibrating in the after-image
their fixity has made, since the flesh tries helplessly
        to preserve such stillness:
a toy model of Pisa
        stirs in the million-watt sun
on the Piazza, the Florentines
walk about in purple tunics
    as whimsical as their tall crenelated towers;
I see Siena shake in the sun, a white façade
        blazing with immense beginnings.
So this Renaissance was a third thing,
        different from the Greek, or the Gothic,
imitating, only to be more itself –
a multi-pinnacled and curious city.

It must be that the kinds of beauty are infinite;
        though we have tried only a few.
I think of the courtiers and 'portraits of young men'
        so plentiful in the galleries,
gentlemen, as there are none now, and those who could command,
        – the condottieri and cavalieri, in arms
            or simply holding a city in the hand –
they no longer exist, Italy
might be a new race, a new people,
as they in their turn were different
        from the Romans they so admired.
            The bawling Italian
in rags, with democratic manners, is certainly a strange curator
of such records: the fees in the museums
are higher than in France, and the guides
one hears everywhere, vulgar in their methods.

Communism is on the walls VOTA COMUNISTA,
        P.C.I., the names of politicians:
though unlike the loud inscriptions
of France, they seem to be the emotions of people.
If it were only an experiment
        I would be glad to see them try it,
but this trial will be permanent, and will erase
the past even more than wars
        or time have been able to do.

The new order, if it is an order,
comes out of economics, as Marx foretold it
        (as the Parthenon did not, nor the cathedrals)
        – it is the culture of industrialism:
'mass production', wealth without mind
to lead it, the shape of things
obeying the laws of Smith and Ricardo (or Marx & Engels
        in desperate countries).
This is even apparent in Florence and Rome,
        as everywhere;
though Italy, agricultural perforce,
has been somewhat backward in beginning –
        Rapallo is 'completely changed' after ten years,
        and here they have 'fenced off' the ruins.
So that what violent politics
and the one-party system may add or take away
makes little difference, will leave no monuments.
The ruins of department stores
        will not impress, in days to come,
as these colonnades do, nor will they stand
before the tourist with dignity and order.

65

I am sure the Italians would trade in Santa Croce
    (with all the bones that are in it)
for a row of comfortable Duplex houses
    on the outskirts of Montreal.
It's the one against the other. And where do we stand?
We, we are not given the choice.
We are a principle in ourselves,
    a foreign body in those suburbs;
building something in the mind only, whose shape, dim
and white, trembles and becomes solid sometimes –
    the one good line in a poem.

66 *Rome*

The present is all too present
and the past all too past:
streetcars and Roman crowds, a monstrous static
          of old echoes and new noise.
I cannot hear my own heartbeat,
how should I hear what falls
from the columns of the Twelve Gods
or the hoarse whispers that grow like moss
on the stumps of the Rostra?
Rome was not built in a day, but a day is enough
once it is over, to make an end to Rome.
Nothing has power that was only power
when it lived and had its will; only the power
that is married to beauty survives. Virgil was not satisfied
with his epic when he died, nor Marc Aurelius
          that he was wise.
We may learn from this how the hours should be adorned
               with leaves
and the columns of days garlanded.

67

This is Rome, where they have dumped together
the Egyptian lions, the old circus, Aphrodite
        and the saint with a bloody stone in his hand.
The Vatican has them all, all the Greeks
with frog leaves over the penis
        (Catholic retouchings
            on pre-Christian marble) –
lousy restorations: excepting the Capitoline's
        magnificent torsos.

The Greeks had an easy mastery,
hundreds of hands, unknown,
        each better than a Michelangelo.
So too, the primitives of Siena, and makers of glass
        and of pointed arches,
where minor craftsmen could be as true and perfect
as a Greek stele –
making the epic, church of Mary.
After which came the third, different,
        with signatures, 'the high Italian';
weak in the knees, brief, but different.
It could hardly outlive the short span
        of the life of Rafaello.
Pompous from the beginning, feeding the ego
        of rich bastards
(the Pitti Palace, 'the wealthiest ever built
        by a private citizen')
and the ego of over-praised artists.

You find a technique, perfect it,
    and in a few years exhaust it.
Ostentation, in the power to do it, follows,
sickening the stomach.
    (And shall we speak of 'l'Arte Moderna'?)
Rome has them all, on the same ash heap,
a metamorphosed mountain, of all strata,
diastrophized into a single ruin,
time's gift and condemnation
    to ignorance and thick-fingered incapacity.

Look at Rome, look at what they have done.
Learn what we do not do,
what we must learn to begin to do,
    and to avoid.

68

Until these letters came I had not known
                how far we had gone
over the sea, the broken crags
and ruins, empty death's heads
of forgotten vigour:
        hambones of the saints,
the spearholes of gladiators,
and the parched remains of St. Cecilia's hair.
But you, sweet children of light, my friends,
        whose letters come by post,
are all earnest and alive,
write, asking where I am, what I have seen
and make me know how lonely
and isolated we have been among the ruins.
The past is something one learns and contemplates
        only to make the present a diamond
as hard as the Duomo of Siena,
brilliant in all facets.
To be torn from these roots is to be dying.
But I would rather have my friend's new poem
        than all the Coliseum,
which is a blood-stained stable, fallen in ruin,
and your kind letters, than all the sculptured words
        in all the crumbling friezes.

v. *What Greece Has Given*

69

Coming back to it all, we know it is more of a miracle
than the sea suggests:
        what the Greeks did, the Italians.
'I don't know if it is because I am Greek,' said
              the young man on the packet,
'but the sea seems bluer,
        the sky bluer than anywhere.'
A touch of nostalgia. And we know, we know
what made the Greeks a nation
of Lotos-Eaters, and the Italians Sybarites
  – war, and civil war, and centuries of serfdom –
but what made them 'the Greeks', we do not know.

Michael tells me
that there will be a renaissance.
But the power is in America, the new Rome.
If we could find out the secret
of these white rocks
         and hand it on to 'big business'
and 'the common man', America would know –
                for 3000 years at least.
But could they ever understand it?
About virtue? The qualities of character?
Or to talk like Socrates?
The sea rinses its mouth and says nothing.
The waves act as if they did not remember.

70

We have seen bits of this marble
 scattered over all the cities of Europe:
how could it be entire? What Greece has given,
and been robbed of, was so much
 they have left nothing for themselves –
 a beggared people, cheating the tourists
on every menu, smiling insidiously,
 living now without cleanness, without order,
surrounded by deserts, the pinkish-white mountains
 parched by the sun,
that one must cross, to Delphi, to Mycenae,
to the cape over the sea at Sunion.

Time and the wars have destroyed it all, but the Acropolis
standing there, crumbling with infinite slowness,
 in the sunlight,
is all that it ever was, will be, until the last speck
of the last stone is swept away by the gentle wind.
Strange, that a few fragile, chalky, incomplete blocks of marble,
 worn away by time, thievery, and gunpowder,
should be enough, and all that we have come for,
to erect in the mind the buildings
 of the Greeks who lived here, and their city –
akro-polis against the blue sky of heaven.
I have said of the sculptures, such people
will never again be, it is more
 than we can really believe in.

Shall we ever again see such buildings? Heaven
        seemed near then so that the hand could touch it.
But we have the light years,
                the immeasurable solitudes.
I sit here, drinking in sunlight
from the clean candid marble,
        thinking the thoughts of Plato,
of Solon, and the perfect republic.

71

And strange, that as we have approached the sun, the
source of light,
time bearing against us, in Spain, in Italy,
we have seen less light in faces, poverty everywhere,
dearth and drouth, which they have learned how to suffer;
the centuries against us, where the brightness blazed once,
ten centuries, five centuries earlier;
and now we are in Greece, the centre,
the poorest place in Europe, where the begging
of infants and women is most importunate.
In the dry mountains,
in the desert, we hear of olives, and sweet fruit,
but everywhere see only open hands, and eyes
turned to the paradise birds, the tourists.
Athens is a stinking agora, with the white Acropolis
behind it.
The sea passage was mild, though filthy,
in steerage quarters, with young tourists
and poor Greeks –
the thin old lady who lost her shoe
in the midnight scuffle,
the old man with long moustaches, standing expressionless.
These Greeks have no visible relation
to the amphora makers, or the bodies in marble,
so neatly combed and aristocratic. The past belongs
to no one people
more than to another; it is a semantic error
to assume that since they have lived and multiplied here
for 3,000 years they have any resemblance ...

Wars have destroyed
not only the temples but the people,
    the destroyers have moved forward
to the next circumference, wider but thinner
acres of cultivation: here in Greece
    was the centre, the beginning of light.
We have come a long way, in the ascent, climbing
around the coils of error, to these ruins,
stumps of paradise.
    No, my people,
we are not golden birds, are as poor as you are;
but take these miserable drachmas
as tokens of our companionable despair.

72

Having come to find in old Europe
  the cities and temples plural (according to Pound)
and the statuary, and the living dead, their places
  remarkable in memory
(preserved by unimportant people, inhabited by tenement
  dwellers),
we have found little, soon almost forgotten,
and the images that live, continually in the mind,
are not of the arts at all,
  but of people:
figures of black-garbed women
  somewhere in Spain,
weaving hats on the stoops of houses,
  système artisanale of 1750;
the friendly communists in France
who were pleased because we ate cheese as they did, by the water,
  and the boys had guessed 'an American professor'
because I read a book
  and 'marked it with a pencil';
or the women of Italy, the women of Greece –
a thin old lady, nodding to and fro in the autobus,
in the heat of the day, with the bags and the watermelon;
or the young men in Corinth, who asked us
  'how to come to America';
the Italian soldier, going home to his family, hopeful,
telling me about the crops there, looking forward to supper;
or the blind vine-grower near Poitiers
who told us the difficulties
      of keeping up the vineyards
    ('the gov't promises to help but does not help');
many others, all people
who had a way of suffering, that was their character.

The arts have been important
    because their fiction worked upon
        the needs of people: the Byzantine Virgin
with the sad dark boy, the great figures of athletes.
   These made men understand, made them strong,
        or taught them grace.
We also have suffering to deal with.
        Can America learn
what Europe needs?
Learn to distrust governments and those in power ...
        Use our millions
to give the older peoples a means to live ...
Buy the olives and currants
    of Greece, the wines of France,
        the dairy products of Denmark;
make those on the land self-sufficient
to keep off the rat-tooth of the ideologue
        – better than tanks and artillery.
Money for schools, money for manufactures,
to keep mobs and their demagogues
        from getting control in the cities.

These nations
again themselves, more or less at ease
        though not up to our standard
                (of living)
may begin to have time
        for freedom,
for the arts, for music, the usual songs.
Now are too impoverished,
       have nothing but their faces
to give us, as images of their companionable despair.

73

I do not think we shall ever again
have great buildings. Temples and churches
built to please or placate a god
were once the occupation of a whole society
led by that superstition. The private dwelling,
or edifice of utility, no matter how pretentious
      – the Pitti Palace, Chambord, Versailles –
is always an atrocity,
      like a much-bejewelled dowager.
Can we find a new symbol
for all those processes
of which we are still a part?
Not until we have become perfectly accustomed
to the invention of elementary machines.

74

But we have seen the country people,
an old man and a younger,
the boy with his arm around the elder's neck,
and a spectre-thin woman with a bundle,
   fragile bones under delicate skin,
    dark-eyed, long-suffering,
and men of fine character, with long moustaches,
      quiet, thoughtful,
and women working in the fields,
   the arms moving beautifully at their labour –
among the olive trees, among the grape vines,
rocky soil, dry, the farms poor and infertile,
but the people patient, inured to suffering, weather-beaten,
indifferent to the capitalist or the communist future,
to the rise or fall of cities,
    arts and civilizations,
indifferent to all but the harvest, war with the soil
    and the weather:
these the peasants, who come before and after.

75

And we have seen Mycenae, that old city
        where Agamemnon lay buried
for 4,000 years while they were farming;
I have thought of them on these hills
        when the water still flowed here,
hoeing and ploughing, breaking the rocks
patiently under the hot sun, by the road
        once patrolled by foot-soldiers –
each *stathmos* still to be seen, dug in the hillside,
and the enemy always beyond in the mountains,
        waiting to destroy.
A clumsy city, built on a hill,
with rickety small streets climbing up to the housedoors
where the pottery stood, the water and wine jugs;
of rough-hewn stone, with simple accommodations;
but powerfully fortified against assault,
against the wars that destroy cities.
They destroyed Mycenae. And the earth covered it all,
and the walls caved in,
        which had been so carefully erected,
by slaves, of course, and the grainstores
        filled by slaves or peasants.
It has all been excavated, to be looked at by tourists,
to be mapped and monographed
        by the French Archaeological Society.
Among the earliest of Greek cities:
        they fought the Trojans.
Then Spartan hoplites marched over these hills,
        over this desert,
to spoil the Athenians, to destroy Athens.
Both sides fought nobly, they say,
bringing honour to their cities.

76

That the labourer deserves to enjoy the product of his labour
is a recent discovery, unknown to history.
          It would never have crossed their minds.
But once seen and spoken, no truth of this kind
can be returned to the chaos
from which, like black diamonds, it was excavated.
There will never be art again
in any society unless it is held together by justice.
Not only that fair dealing is important
          as regards the poor and ignorant peasant
who produces only the perishable
          fruit, meat, and vegetables
we all consume: these and his pains
count of course in human, even animal, terms;
and love, the Christian virtue, has built cathedrals;
but justice is also important
to those above, who must deal out fairly, the bosses
who trade, who manage the state preserves.
The first beauty of all is the beauty of fair dealing
between the seller and those who buy, between the employer
          and those who work.
After this, others come, in a long procession,
maidens carrying flowers, boys with branches,
cattle with hanging udders:
          the marble and music
and 'gold that ennobles life,' *megalanora plouton*
          and the flowers of song.

I have heard that there were gardens in Corinth
where one might enjoy the pleasures of the flesh
and cool water from distant mountains.
The ruins of two theatres and a temple in the Doric style
still mark the place where these pleasures were once enjoyed.

77

Good art is the record of a good society.
A society without art has proved itself corrupt
by absolute demonstration.
We must look to our ethics.

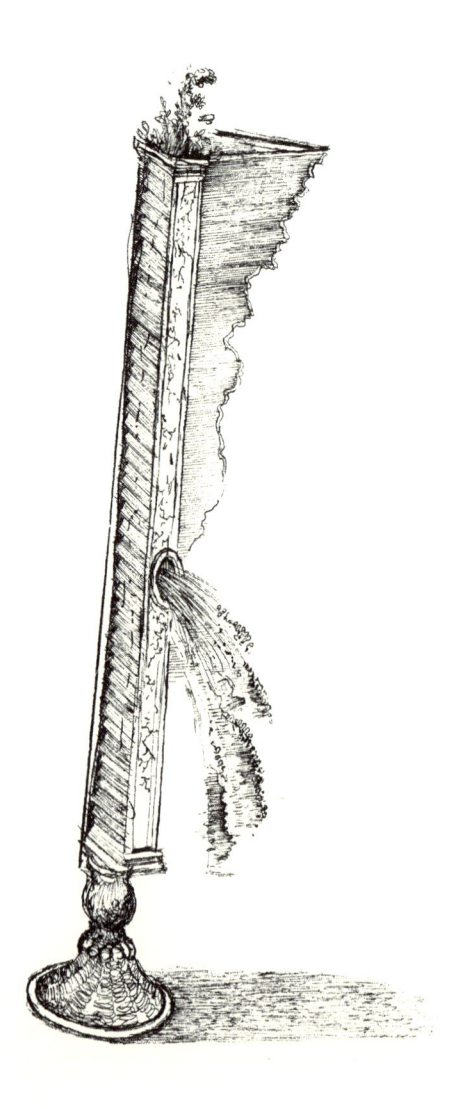

78

Even the remnant of a work of art,
        like the broken temple at Delphi,
has an obvious ethical content.
I agree with Ruskin.
Not that the good can be easily defined:
there are many forms
        of activity, conditions of character.
Evil is whatever denies or destroys
        a human capability.
This temple is very beautiful
        because it is a kind of personal
record, the report of a man; one would have loved
        to live with such people.

79

The forms of beauty are many.
I liked those goats on the mountain,
the hillside covered with olive trees,
               and the little children
playing in the villages.
        A Turkish sword-hilt, very elaborate,
and a Byzantine church filled with mosaics,
            are too a manifestation
of infinite creativity (of nature, the gods in us)
which has made our intelligence,
each particular and simple,
the everyday person we live with
who grows to flower by loving and living.

80

But remember that it is the mess we perpetuate
    (Westerman said: A History
of Human Stupidity) that shapes us,
as well as whatever virtues.
A continent is mountainous with petrifactions:
the jewels and bones of the Vatican,
the putridities of contemporary Catholicism
        (the young are eating the sh—t
            which history has evacuated,
       intellectuals of Paris,
           intellectuals of London);
or Sartre's desperate affiance
    with the Russian church of humanitarianism
that kills without mercy
because their unction is sick with their hatred;
and Picasso's conformity
    after a life of cubist ungovernability.
All this will be passed on to our children,
         a heritage
born of asceticism, born of our guilts.
    Shall we continue murdering our children?
or hanging them on the hillsides?
If we must transmit servilities,
    let us throw in a few seeds of freedom.

81

We saw a village on a mountain
    as we crossed the Gulf of Corinth,
a lonely place in the dry hills, with greenery around it
        and dusty olive trees.
I thought: They live there, isolated and poor,
I imagine they work together to sustain one another,
all suffer, or all enjoy what they gain together.
But on nearer observation I could see the walls
    and separate houses of the village,
with all the signatures of property.
            There, as in every city
they have the prosperous and the needy,
and some of the dogs get more than the poorest inhabitants.
Every inch of the crooked land is measured
    (a problem for the surveyor)
tagged with a deed of sale, a date and an owner;
    and though the whole village, flayed by the sun,
must hide in the rocks like a cicada,
it is divided against itself. All Greece
is like this. A civil war has rent it,
    the infection
of our world burns in its entrails.

In the Orthodox churches they also have the entablature
and a somewhat Corinthian capital.
The Gothic arch never penetrated this far;
ornate, excessively, but old Greek still,
and the music was excellent.
    (Who knows how the ancient really sounded?)
I suppose it is better to see the past live
in over-decorativeness than not at all,
as the cathedral
has contributed something even to the Empire State building.

83

As for democracy, it is not just the triumph
        of superior numbers,
but that everyone, continually,
should think and speak the truth.
What freedom is there in being counted among the cattle?
The first right I want is to be a man.
It takes a little courage.
The plain truth, I say, not a few comfortable formulas
that conceal your own special lies;
the simple facts everybody knows
are so, as soon as you bring them to the light.
Democracy is this freedom, this light
shining on the human mind,
                  light
in faces, actions –
as the Greeks once carved it in these stones.

84

By the red cliffs at Vouliagmeni
where the wind blows in from the islands,
         from Samos, Chios, and Mytilene
no matter how filthy the land is,
the sea is clean and the wind
         cool, scrubbing the sea cliffs.
The man on the donkey is bawling 'Retsina,'
the only wine they drink here,
         a naphthaline mixture
my stomach refuses; but the grapes are 'as fine as any
         on the Italian peninsula.'
Forty thousand Greeks want to go to America
              (said the man at the Embassy),
of these we have met a number; this land has nothing to offer.
We have seen a lot of Europe,
keeping our eyes open,
the poor villages of France, the pueblos of Spain,
         poverty in Italy, poverty in Greece;
and England, of course, still the best corner of Europe.
It seems that we have come all this distance
to discover the virtues of America (the continent, Canada
         being a good part of it); call it a prejudice,
but minus the Coca-Cola, minus the damn advertisements,
today the land and the people
with the best working intelligence, alert and practical,
not lacking in generosity, and the will to improvement,
not lacking the social virtues;

 give them an elementary education
 in what makes a product permanent,
   as well as useful; i.e. some sign
of the conscious life, which they have obliterated
     by too much action,
as in the case of the obtuse and stupid
    businessman
      (one could go on with the subject),
but compared to the European
whose entire glory is in monuments
    useless for the purpose of living,
the people impoverished, unpractical, uneducated,
the commercial crooks getting all that they can
     out of an archaic system
(American aid going into the pockets
    of bureaucrats everywhere),
the New World is every bit as good
     as the immigrants imagine
(40,000 applicants,
   of whom ten per cent will be lucky),
where wages are high and the standard of living
    goes up with increasing manufacture,
where the instalment plan makes sure
   you can buy some of the overproduction
(all but the military waste, all but the capital glut).

If I had my choice, I would live in Ancient Athens
first of all; but in modern Athens not at all:
40,000 Greeks have decided
that the old source of light
is the darkest place in Europe;
                light moves in waves
out of the centre, to its new circumference,
whether to multi-national America
        or the new barbarism of the Russians.
                What new periplum
will surround the world,
war, or better, time alone, can decide.

This was written at Vouliagmeni
        by the sea, the wind blowing seaward.

Finis

85

We have come to Ithaca, Ulysses' island.
I imagine that when the hero came here
                and had settled his affairs,
he was glad to have left behind
the foreign magic, foreign women,
                and the long delays.
They write about Ithaca that it is 'a small island
                off the coast of Greece';
actually, we have already been one hour
                trying to get past it.
A bigger place than one might have expected. Ulysses,
                if he landed here,
would have had a good week
                of hard walking to reach the end.
But this was his home. I guess he did some good
for his people (as much as in his so-called cleverness
                he could) –
replenished his reserves, aided civilization –
when he got back, remembering his voyage,
remembering Troy's ruin.

86

The green hills of Italy, after the white rocks of Greece.
It was, after all, a desert:
         'The farther north you go,'
said the two teachers from Lebanon,
'the more decency you'll find.'
'All Greeks are dishonest,' said the Greek.
But civilization travelled this way,
it's as if it had left the land behind
         a scorched desert, exhausted
of all possibility, by so much effort.
We had travelled a long time
to get to the middle of it,
         and now, returning
we seem to be going again
            towards it:
'Vous avez pris le flambeau,' said the Frenchman
         speaking of America.
This circle
      has moved
            to and from the beginning,
always going towards that
         vanishing light.

87

Beginning with so much art and arrogance
the search for the past has ended
it seems, on the rocks of the present –
    islands stricken by catastrophe, impoverished
                                  Italy and its people.
The girl with the green eyes was beautiful
in the train, explaining about the schools,
and the voices in Rome heard in the street
    and outside the window
ran up and down like mandolines and fiddles:
soft, delicate Italians, swift in movement,
    faces as in the paintings of the Cinquecento.
Poverty isn't everything,
when there is such wealth
    in personal behaviour,
passed on no doubt from generation to generation
like the art of every city
    to all its *cittadini*.
We are leaving for Venice,
    the bells of Rome are ringing.

88

In Venice, where the sea taught them mobility
                             and the art of mixing,
the arches are curved and pointed
upwards, with a few birds or a bunch of flowers
               at the top.
There are 200, or 154, columns
            (depending on the guide)
                      in the architecture of St. Mark's
and the Ducal Palace contains all the art
     (so much beauty in detail
        you would think it grew there,
     as in a field, where every leaf has some order)
from Giotto to Tiepolo – spoiled,
        after G. Bellini.
However, where the procurators gathered
under the file of arches in the Piazzale
are now the high-class shop windows
         filled with tourist bric-à-brac,
and on the Rialto
where the merchants of Venice did their business
the pestilence of the new commerce
        that neither builds nor decorates
Duomo or Accademia, trails to the Venetian ghetto
where we stayed, and thought of these things.

89

In mountains, which are the white-flecked breakers
of the land, so huge the eyes become ocean-hollows,
we see what dimensions these things aspire to.
Beyond imitation. Yet whatever is essential
                                    to humanity,
is to be seen in a few mountainous endeavours –
                  a Leonardo, an Aristotle.
As in Switzerland, it is efficiency
              which the mountains have given
for emulation: freedom, and relief from the savagery
                    of wars.
In these Alps you will find
tiny blueberries – that we picked by St. Gotthard –
              and Swiss watches,
both very excellent.
            The size of things
is not to be measured, but by the imagination.

90

And so we fell out of the heights
into the billowing apron
          of Germany.
The sunrise was beautiful, white clouds after.
This scenery, we said, is better than any
we have seen on our voyage; clouds are necessary,
    even when they are muggy,
        like the German mind:
a peasant people, absurdly commonplace, practical.
'Yet they have done more
    for the world, than any nation.'
And also later, seeing the clouds like porridge
over the pointed steeples, and feeling the wind bite,
I knew what Goethe
    was glad to get away from.
We work hard in our northern countries
for the few obvious things that matter.
        We have so little
of the warm sun; it will be a long time
before we can be as easy, and graceful, and lazy
    as the Latins are,
who are familiar with all those marble capitals.
'I know this country,' I said,
    looking at the sky, in Germany,
'this is already home.'

91

We have ended as we started, looking at churches
                 and Euclidean cemeteries,
from Frankfurt-among-the-ruins
to the shattered face of Reims,
                 an image in unstill water.
On one of the battlefields of the Marne
you picked berries
while I kicked up the nose of an exploded shell
                 by the white hollow of a dugout, 1918.
The berries were good, red and sweet,
                 after thirty years,
growing among the quiet remains;
                 time is trying hard to level
the trenches and shell-holes a war left behind.
Have I said enough
that wars destroy, not only the living bodies
                 but all the good that men create?
Two hundred and sixty-seven shells
                 fell on the Cathedral of Reims.
The Dom of Frankfurt-am-Main
stands in a level plain, of rubble,
                 where once were the fine old buildings of that city.
All Europe has been laid waste, we have seen
                 what the wars have left,
from old Mycenae to new Mainz, we have seen the ruins;
little stands that we could still praise,
                 save cathedrals,
scarred remnants of the Europe that we came to find.

92

Here where it is all sea and sky, it doesn't matter
what monuments on land are crumbling
the past left behind, or that since then everything
        has deteriorated;
it does not matter that Europe is little more now
    than an accumulation of bad habits,
        or that their heritage is wasted;
the present begins with nothing, has everything
before it; we are lucky
to be able to go back
to where nothing is revered or old
and no excellence an obstacle, or much better
    than what we ourselves can do. Our power
is like the clear sight of new races
with many aims, many desires untried and unsatisfied,
        unlike the Europeans,
who are tired of it all, or helpless, or exhausted.
We have lots to do, we in America,
        who know that there is no end
to the journey, no end to the joy
we can bring to many, before the power in us
becomes entire, and civilization (that's the word) is
        again accomplished.

93

We ran into a heavy sea, leaving England,
fog, and unshapely waves, scythed cruelly by the wind;
the torrent passing under us then,
              black, fearful,
was like a curtain suddenly; the awful ocean
          closed on the continent,
blotted out Europe, the fortified walls of Cherbourg,
lights of refineries, helpless houses:
a luminous green ran under us, streaming, swirling
– I saw as in a mirror, through a manhole,
a small fishing smack tossed to and fro on the water.
Can they go on living?
      The sea has washed out
everything I have written, the fiction of temporaneity:
we are back with the real, the uncreated
chaos of ocean,
which will not stop to spare us
            a regret for all we have lost and forgotten.

94

Today it is cool and refreshing.
    The sea is almost still,
ice-bright, hard and sun-glazed. Europe is gone.
    One begins to have some perspective.
        Like the dead, we remember
the symbolic events that mattered:
        the red roofs of Chartres
as seen from the cathedral
    where the schoolchildren sang in unison
sitting at lunch on the green; a boy we befriended in Spain
who wanted to learn from a grammar
    how to speak the English tongue;
a priest on a bicycle; the Italian girls on the train
who said with their eyes that 'love
is better than money'; the young man in the church
at Lancaster, and the woman who prayed
in Mainz: all these are remembered
in the first effort to return, to relive in memory
what was too little comprehended. Life, like poetry,
can only be understood through comparison, what results
is the perfect, unchanging essence,
        an eidolon of the good.

95

The sea retains such images
    in her ever-unchanging waves;
for all her infinite variety, and the forms,
inexhaustible, of her loves,
she is constant always in beauty,
    which to us need be nothing more
    than a harmony with the wave on which we move.
All ugliness is a distortion
of the lovely lines and curves
    which sincerity makes out of hands
    and bodies moving in air.
Beauty is ordered in nature
    as the wind and sea
shape each other for pleasure; as the just
know, who learn of happiness
    from the report of their own actions.

96

    Incredible how the water came crashing this morning
                in torrents over the bows.
Infinite, unsatisfied, the storm-driven waves
chaotically rose, sometimes culminating
by chance in such wind-shattered forms
as only the Alps or Himalayas
              suggest by analogy, but vaster
because they moved, and appeared out of nowhere,
              and fell massively over us.
The ship rose and fell, groaning
        and crying like a kitten; all the passengers
were white again, many stayed where they had slept,
others came up just to look at the thing.
              It came out of the night
and had no end. We were all helpless
before its immeasurable volume and violence.
This was certainly beauty, but of a kind not desirable
to man, who looks for happiness, and comfort
              in a world he can control.
The sea in itself is more than he can take
              with any real advantage.
The way for us is to keep close enough to the shore
in order to domesticate these forces,
            using the sea always
to enrich our ports and inland cities.

97

Despite its size and sublimity, one comes to realize
that we are not really interested in the ocean,
which for all its variety
    is an empty desolation
        (I wanted to weep
looking into the night, into the cold solitude,
echoing what we would bury within us
        and utterly forget).
One would want to see people, a ship, or islands,
    to bring joy to these waters –
the friendly islands
    of St. Pierre and Miquelon,
the rough coast of Gaspé.
On the land, rain and rivers
    are good for agriculture,
but the sea cannot be planted, is no place for cities.

98

On this ship there are several Italians and a few Greeks
going to America, emigrants, the raw matter
of democracy; Europe sends us its people.
They are looking forward
to higher standards of living, better pay,
but not a life of less toil than they have known.
In the factories, or on the farms, they get the hardest
share of the labour.
Welcome! It is really a matter
of making a living, after all, this thing we call success,
whether for a man or for a nation;
though it will take a little time
before a material civilization
discovers the language of its self-applause.
They will find America tough, not rotten,
the evil there as positive as the good.
And they will have very far to go.
We ourselves are going to America. We have been going
a long time. When we get there
we may find ourselves surprised, and just as hard-worked,
tired, and happy, as they are.

99

And so we have arrived.
It narrows into the thin St. Lawrence.
Yet a river with a city inside it,
        with a thousand islands,
as Cartier found it,
as Cabot discovered (I saw his face
        in the Ducal Palace in Venice).
We have had our physical heroes,
and are also a nation
built in the middle of water.
Somehow a bigger place than we left it:
a country with certain resources,
        and a mind of its own, if lacking hunger.
The mountains of Gaspé doze, reclining,
        in the air vacant as morning.
At home, there will be faces full of this daylight,
        blank maybe, but beautiful.
Getting started is never easy.
We have work to do.
        Europe is behind us.
            America before us.

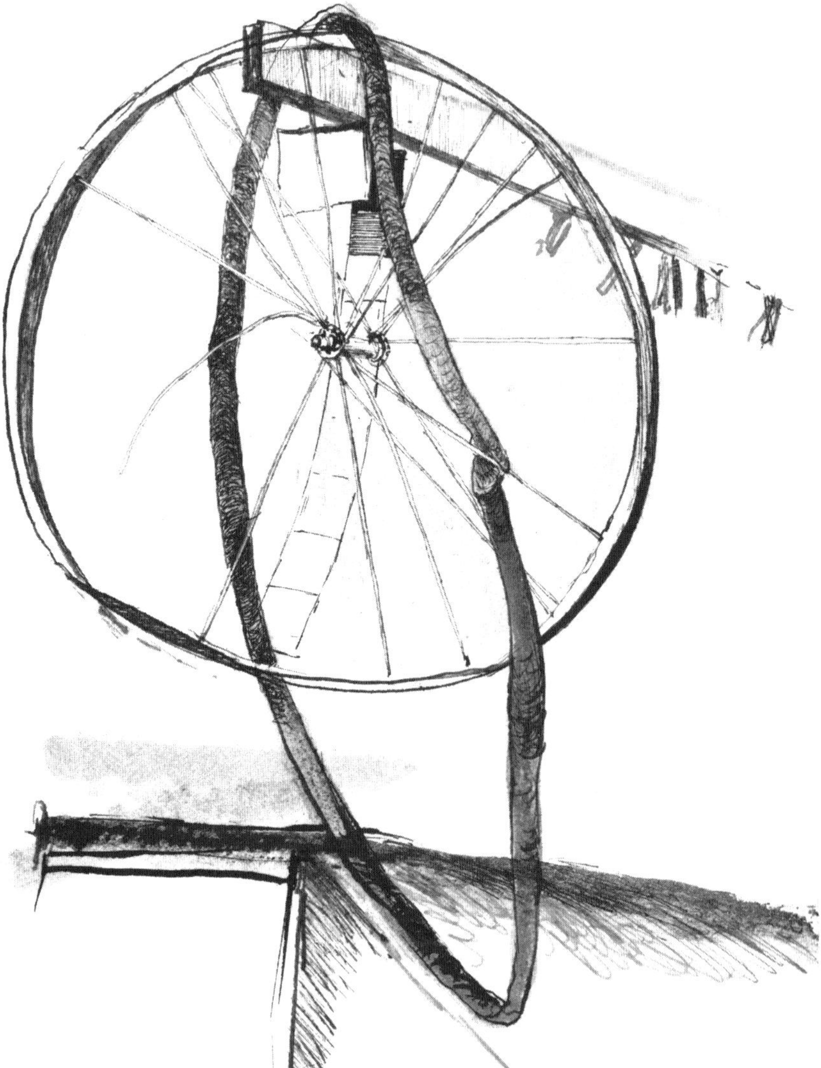

Europe – The history as afterword

Europe, though dated 1954 in the first edition, appeared, in fact, in the spring of 1955[1], and was distributed to readers and reviewers in the early summer of that year. It bore the maverick imprint of Laocoön Press[2] with (CONTACT) bracketed within that imprint, and was Dudek's first major book of poetry of substantial length, following on the more modest heels of his two Ryerson Press collections, *East of the City* (1946) and *The Searching Image* (1952), and Contact's own *Twenty-Four Poems* (1952).

On the page facing the title, a note explained that the 'poem' was also a 'journal', and that 'references to persons and events

---

1 A copy of the book in my possession and inscribed to Irving Layton reads: 'For Irving – one of the first two copies of this book to reach Canada, April 5, 1955. Louis Dudek.'

2 Laocoön Press was the short-lived but overt expression of Dudek's and Layton's 'separatist' tendencies *vis-à-vis* Contact Press, and what was, apparently, their unhappiness with Raymond Souster's susceptibility to American influences, notably that of Cid Corman, editor of the American literary magazine, *Origin*. The other title that appeared under its imprint was Layton's *The Long Pea-Shooter* (1954) which, however, unlike *Europe*, gave Montreal as its place of publication, and neither mentioned Contact Press, nor, as became the custom with other Contact Press books, gave Souster's address in Toronto as its place of origin.

The Laocoön reference derives from the work of an American humanist, Irving Babbitt (1865-1933), who advocated a return to a more rigorous classical tradition in criticism and literature. He initiated a movement called New Humanism. One of his works, *The New Laokoön* (1910), influenced Dudek's thinking while he was a student at Columbia University in the 1940s.

... are at times coloured to suit the poem's purpose.'[3] The note[4] also served to signal what would become Dudek's lifelong concern with the search for truth in poetry, and his equally long-lived penchant for the didactic. Clearly he was staking an early claim to a place in Utopia.

The true beginnings of *Europe* lie in the idea of the cultural pilgrimage that Dudek undertook to the Continent in 1953. He had completed his second year of teaching in the English Department of McGill University – a performance, one adds from personal memory, keen and constant in its reminders of our debt to the great process of European civilization.[5] Two years earlier, while preparing to return to Canada from New York, and reacting against what he perceived as the narrowing and provincial vision of John Sutherland's 'nativism', Dudek

---

3 How much of a faithful 'journal' of things seen, people met, and places visited the poem turned out to be is evidenced in the contents of the letter Dudek wrote to Souster on 11 June 1953 from San Sebastian in Spain. For example, Southampton, Lancaster, London and Paris, which are mentioned specifically in the letter, and clearly impressed Dudek during his tour, became elements in the poem. At that point in his journey, Dudek noted that he was a day away from Pamplona, reference to which, of course, occurs in Section 55.
4 The full text of the note reads: 'References to persons and events in this journal are at times coloured to suit the poem's purpose. For the relation of inaccuracy to truth in poetry the reader is referred to Aristotle's *Poetics*. As for being didactic, Plato teaches, at the end of the *Republic*, that we had better be, if we want a place in utopia.'
5 As an example of Dudek's deep-seated interest in, and commitment to, European culture; one points to his supremely successful course called 'The Great Writings of Europe' which he established as an English Department offering at McGill University and which he taught for many years. One of the texts, I recall, was Emery Neff's influential book, *A Revolution in European Poetry*. Dudek had studied with Neff at Columbia University.

had said in a letter to Souster, 'Who in hell cares whether it's native or not? And do we want to be natives forever?...' And a little further on in the same letter while defending Katherine Mansfield who had been criticized in *Northern Review* for having 'belonged to the European tradition,' Dudek had exclaimed, 'We've got to *belong to the European tradition!!!!*' He set out, therefore, to see and experience for himself the stunning reality of Europe and its monumental past. The intellectual baggage that Dudek took on this voyage was crammed with the great writings of Europe, while, slung over his shoulder, he carried the powerful example of Ezra Pound.

The first mention of *Europe* occurs in Dudek's letter of 11 June 1953 to Souster in which, at the bottom of a sprawling two-page, hand-written account he says, 'I've written 150 lines of poetry on this trip already, believe it or not!!' This was followed, upon Dudek's return home, by another reference to the poem in a letter of 22 September 1953. Dudek said:

> I've got a burden of a poem, 1,400 lines, written all over Europe, entitled EUROPE. It should be published, but I have no money, so that will wait.

But the wait was not to be a long one. In the summer of 1954, Stephanie Dudek wrote from New York[6] to express her

---

6 In a letter dated 9 June 1954, Stephanie Dudek wrote: 'I'm delighted that *Europe* will be out so soon and so cheaply. And $1000! – lord – for once in the last fifteen years you won't need to watch the next penny. How wonderful!' On 25 May 1954, Dudek had written to Souster to say that he had put *Europe* into production. He said: '*Europe*, also, is in production. Having it done in England by Niemojowski & Bernarczyk (Officina Poetarum et Pictorum) for 130 pounds, equivalent to $370. I'd have to sell 185 copies at $2 to pay for the edition; but I could make about $400 if the 500 sold out.' At this point there is no mention of the thousand dollars, the source of

happiness over a windfall of a thousand dollars which meant that the poem could proceed to publication. The evidence suggests that Dudek had had his poem in a finished state late in 1953, for he reported to Souster then that he had submitted sections of it to the American editor and fellow poet, Cid Corman, who in those years was very much an influential presence in the background of Souster's little magazine, *Contact*. It should be added that Corman, with his own literary periodical *Origin*, was an important link between the Contact group in Canada and some of the newer writers emerging on the American scene. Poets like Robert Creeley, Charles Olson, Paul Blackburn, Ted Enslin and Vincent Ferrini, among others. Although Corman had 'discovered' Canada through Dudek, the two were not overly fond of each other's work, and Corman quickly took a liking to Layton, working actively to promote him in the United States with the writers clustered around *Black Mountain Review*, and in the pages of *Origin*. Corman returned the submitted sections of *Europe*, prompting Dudek to explode in his letter to Souster on 25 January 1954:

> That sap Corman sent back some of my 'Europe' which he had *asked* for (I wdn't bother otherwise) with a page and a half of his shite criticism gratuitous into the bargain.

And when Souster took up *Europe*'s cause with Corman, the latter wrote on 17 February 1954 in a conciliatory but unyielding vein, saying:

> You may be right in your feeling of Dudek's poem. Perhaps in toto it seems more of an achievement and, I suppose, it is.

---

which remains obscure. When published, *Europe* sold for $2 as Dudek had envisaged.

Late in May of that year, Dudek reported confidently to Souster that, 'Europe, also [in addition to *Trio*[7]] is in production at last. Having it done in England ...' and on 24 September he would write:

> Proofs of *Europe* arrived Friday & I mailed them out today. It is still good to me. The delay was caused by moving of the printing house twice, forced by the law.

It would be April of 1955 before the first two copies of the book reached Canada, and of these, the second was inscribed to Irving Layton, who recorded the following complimentary reaction. In his letter of 28 August 1955, Layton wrote to Dudek:

> Your *Europe* is a very fine book, but it is badly disfigured by intelligibility and passion. There's not that dylanish blood-and-thunder rhetoric, the macphersonish privacies, the cormanish pseudo-profundities: it lacks entirely the charm of Olson's gift, prose wrapped up in curlers, – it shares, alas, the defects of Blake's 'Songs of Experience'; it happens, alas, to be poetry. You ought to be severely censured for this. Had you thrown in a riddle here and there, combined as Rexroth did in his book penis and politics, whores and history, and seasoned the whole melange with an elementary course in oriental

---

7 *Trio: First Poems by Gael Turnbull, Phyllis Webb* [and] *E.W. Mandell* (1954) with Mandel's name misspelt [in this connection Dudek writes today: 'This was an error of the students who did the job on a varitype machine. I was trying to *encourage* the poor bastards. Many of the copies were *corrected* by hand.'] was the first important sponsorship by Contact Press through the medium of anthologized collections of the younger poets of the time. In later years there would be *Poets '56* and *New Wave Canada* (1966).

151

metaphysics, had you been Sartrishly bitter, or perverse, or tough, or sophisticated, had you been a more attentive reader of the *New Yorker*, had you in fact simply minded your own business and not published the book at all – you would have been more popular. The kind of concern you have isn't fashionable today; and since you're not an intellectual you take ideas seriously and they are good ideas, but not the kind the world just now wishes to hear about. Besides, since alcohol, sex, and the analyst's couch are the other side of the coin which also has the superscription of commissar-chromium crap most people have forgotten what poetry is all about or intended to be. For myself, when I wish to think of a poet I can put you beside to sort of orientate me, I always think of Shelley. The same purity, the same passion.

In the meantime, Dudek, who in his own words that June had 'spread around about ninety copies of the thing so far' to friends and others in his ever-widening circle, had gone to New York to spend the summer and to await, doubtlessly, the reviews that should begin to appear in the fall.

The reviews were not long in coming and, beginning with the major Canadian newspapers, the reception of the book was good. Privately, E.J. Pratt, William Carlos Williams and others wrote to congratulate Dudek on an admirable achievement; their sentiments became part of the advertising flyer for *Europe*. Pratt thought that the poem was something '... which combines the cerebral and the visceral,' while Williams said that 'The language of it is so simply put down, without pretence, that I am all admiration ...' In the magazines, the reviewer for *Saturday Night* called *Europe* 'a remarkable Canadian work', while Milton Wilson, working earnestly at a longer and more serious discussion of the poem wandered into a controversy when he described it as 'both puzzling and impressive'. He was immediately taken to task by Bob Currie, a Montrealer of polemical disposition who belonged to the *CIV/n*[8] circle of writers and who concluded his counter-attack with the following ringing assertion:

> *Europe* is a powerful poem and an important one. Mr. Wilson's narking remarks about it are irrelevant.

Wilson, startled by Currie's vehemence and, one suspects, puzzled by the word 'narking', attempted to defend his review, but he was also under attack by another individual, a gentleman named Alexander St.-John Swift who had written from Barrie, Ontario, and who took issue with the review in general and, in particular, with Wilson's belief that Dudek's ideas were those of Ezra Pound and that *Europe* 'was simple.' Such was his genuine concern that Wilson decided 'to elaborate on and reconsider seriously what I meant by my too cryptic description of *Europe* as an 'education poem'. He proceeded to write another review of the book in which he treated the poem with greater attention and critical generosity than he had first accorded to it. The truth, however, will out, and it became known before too long that Alexander St.-John Swift was Louis Dudek writing under a pseudonym, and that Milton Wilson had been gently chivvied into giving the poem more notice than he had, perhaps, originally intended. History is silent on whether he ever forgave Currie and Dudek for their bit of literary horseplay.

The question of Ezra Pound and his influence on Dudek became, appropriately enough, an issue for critics at about the time of the publication of *Europe*. Pound, a prisoner of

---

8 *CIV/n* was a little magazine published in Montreal in 1953-1954. Its circle included Aileen Collins and Bob Currie, with Dudek and Layton acting discreetly as grey eminences. The story of *CIV/n* has been told in *CIV/n [:] A Literary Magazine of the 50's*. Edited by Aileen Collins with the assistance of Simon Dardick. Montreal: Véhicule Press, 1983.

153

misguided conscience at St. Elizabeths, a psychiatric hospital in Washington, D.C., had become a huge problem and an embarrassment for the American intellectual community. He had been put away because of his anti-Allied radio broadcasts from fascist Italy during the Second World War. A good part of his fulminating had been aimed at the American government establishment, the banking community, and President Roosevelt. The sense and intention of these broadcasts had been readily interpreted as anti-American, and Pound had been charged with treason, had been found to be mentally incompetent to stand trial, and had been committed to St. Elizabeths. There, however, he refused to be silenced, and a steady stream of his publications poured out in the early 1950s[9] to perplex and assault an already nervous American reading public then in the grip of Senator Joseph McCarthy's witch-hunt investigations aimed at those suspected of anti-American activities. In that climate of uncertainty and suspicion it mattered little that Pound was anti-Marxist. As a matter of fact, Mona Van Duyn, the reviewer for *Poetry* (Chicago), in the only major foreign periodical to review *Europe*, who was inclined to be friendly to the book, concluded by saying that Dudek had been rendered cantankerous in the latter portions of the poem by what Van Duyn felt was the baleful influence of Ezra Pound. It could very well be that being reminded of the celebrated poet/prisoner was enough to prompt a skittish or prudent Van Duyn into saying that,

... I think one might be forgiven for cutting off from his

---

9 *The Letters of Ezra Pound* edited by D.D. Paige came out in 1950; a new edition of his influential *Guide to Kulchur* was published in 1952; and *The Translations of Ezra Pound* and his *Literary Essays* in 1953. Harvard University Press issued Pound's translation of the three hundred 'Odes' of ancient China as *The Classic Anthology Defined by Confucius* in 1954.

[Dudek's] poetry and trying to get passage home on a different boat.
(*Poetry* [Chicago], 88:5:330 Ag 1956)

Dudek, it should be noted, had linked[10] his name with that of Pound, and had followed this up with efforts in *CIV/n*[11] on behalf of Pound's release from St. Elizabeths. Dudek had visited Pound in hospital, admired him as a poet, and recognized his great service to modernism. Undoubtedly, *Europe* had drawn on the friendship between the two men, and gained something from the kind of inspiration that Pound's dedication to literature provided. But *Europe* was a very different kind of work from *The Cantos*, to which it was being superficially compared.

First of all, the case of Ezra Pound, not unlike that of another illustrious exile from America, Henry James, was an example of an imagination driven abroad, and therefore, away from America, by that continent's philistinism and deep-seated lack of understanding of art and for the thinking artist who creates it. Pound, feeling rejected by the ethos of America, rejected it in his own turn. For him there was no going back, except under conditions of the most dreadful duress. Dudek, quite on the contrary, with his democratic spirit (as opposed to Pound's elitist stance) was quite comfortable with the idea of America, and felt exhilarated at the prospect of returning home. He spoke for himself as well as for the immigrants on the ship when he said:

---

10 For a fascinating insight into the Dudek/Pound relationship see *D/k: Some Letters of Ezra Pound*. Montreal: DC Books, 1974. In 1955, on the occasion of Pound's seventieth birthday, Dudek wrote and broadcast a tribute to him on the CBC network which included readings from *The Cantos* and *Hugh Selwyn Mauberley*.
11 The name, *CIV/n* was taken from Pound's dictum: CIV/n [civilization] not a one man job.

>   They will find America tough, not rotten,
>   the evil there as positive as the good.
>   And they will have very far to go.
>   We ourselves are going to America. We have been going
>   a long time. When we get there
>   we may find ourselves surprised, and just as hard-worked,
>   tired and happy, as they are.
>   (*Europe*, Section 98)

Then, also, Pound was seized early on with his idea that the lending of money for interest was an intolerably corrupting process that had entered into history, and which he wanted us to see as a great cultural flux. Usury was the enemy of poetry and the arts, and *The Cantos*, joined to his pamphleteering and his letter writing, became not only a poem but a powerful instrument for waging war in a variety of ways and contexts against the unnatural practice of *usura*. Dudek, on the other hand, was and continues to be a social democrat suspicious of power whether it be political or financial, and believing throughout the poem in the people and their works:

>   You will know by their arts,
>   the fruits of a civilization.
>   Honest minds, like the Communist
>   we met at the plage with his family,
>   do a lot of good to make one confident
>   at least in the ferment
>   within the present; but what people have left
>   or what they are now building
>   speaks from the heart and from the centre
>   of any community,
>   (*Europe*, Section 60)

The gesture here is private, the expectation reasonable, the tone in no way that of a harangue.
   Finally, and this may be the most important difference

between Dudek and Pound: *The Cantos,* fine and sweeping poetry that they are, operate at the same time at the level of public address. They are driven by Pound's obsessions, by his eccentric reading in history, his specialized sense of Western literature, his need to declaim and convince. Thus they become a public task in which the poet's hortatory voice constantly uncovers for us the merits of past civilizations and warns us against our own passive natures. Dudek's *Europe,* on the other hand, is a poem of personal discovery in which a set of private pilgrimages eases us into a sharing of the joys of the middle way. It takes delight in that which is unique and fine, as well as pleasure in what is simply great experience, whether it be the windows of Chartres, a swim at Bordighera, the charm of a boy befriended in Spain. We are guided by the poet's musing voice, and invited to share in the discoveries of the day. And over all, of course, there is the sea, and against it the great names and the great places are as nothing – Kant, Marx, London, the Grand Casino are as nothing.

> Although we have come far
> to see what we have seen, I do not think
>   that we shall ever equal the sea.
> History is really the study of failures,
>   the best buildings
> lack some points of proportion, dimension.
> Only the sea makes her circle perfect.
>   (*Europe,* Section 40)

Only the sea, 'lapping quietly at our feet', but, at the same time the central and all-inspiring presence on whose tide the real and the spiritual voyage of discovery begins; that which becomes the paramount referent, shaping us and, incidentally, moulding our sense of beauty to its own magnificent design. For Dudek, as for Pound – and here the comparison is legitimate and draws the two closer – 'In nature are signatures / needing no verbal tradition' (*Canto* LXXXVII). The work of men, regardless of how powerful has been the sweep of history; how fine the line that we have carved; how much 'art and arrogance' we may have proclaimed; however noble the statement of our imagination; all of these, all are only a counterpoint. For the sea has carried us outward on this 'search for the past', and it is the sea that has taught us that 'All ugliness is a distortion', and it is the sea that will carry us back.

>We have work to do.
>>Europe is behind us.
>>>America before us.
>>>>(*Europe*, Section 99)

Michael Gnarowski

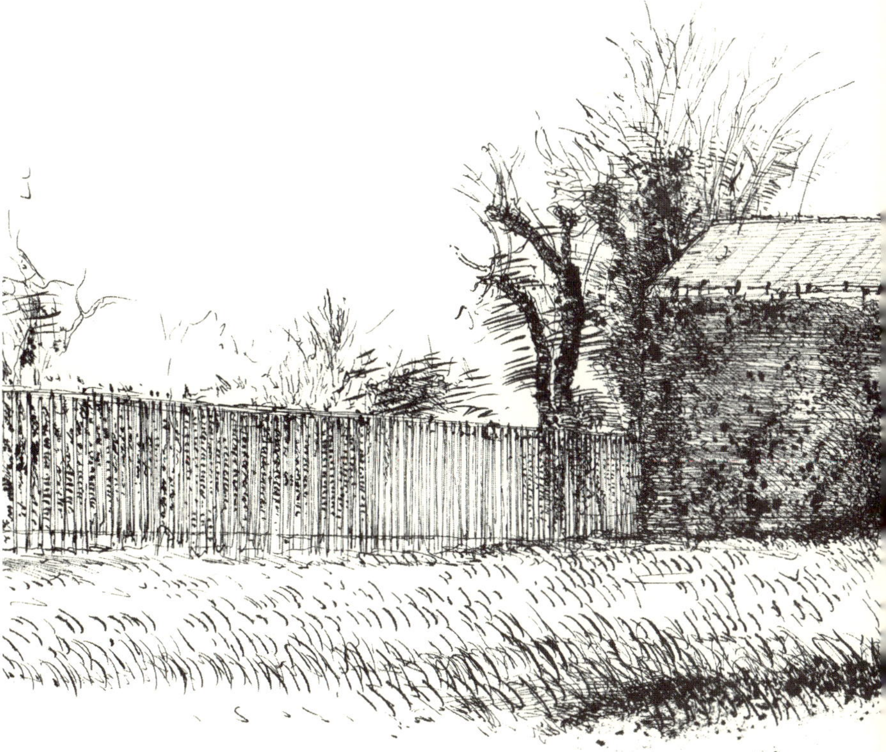

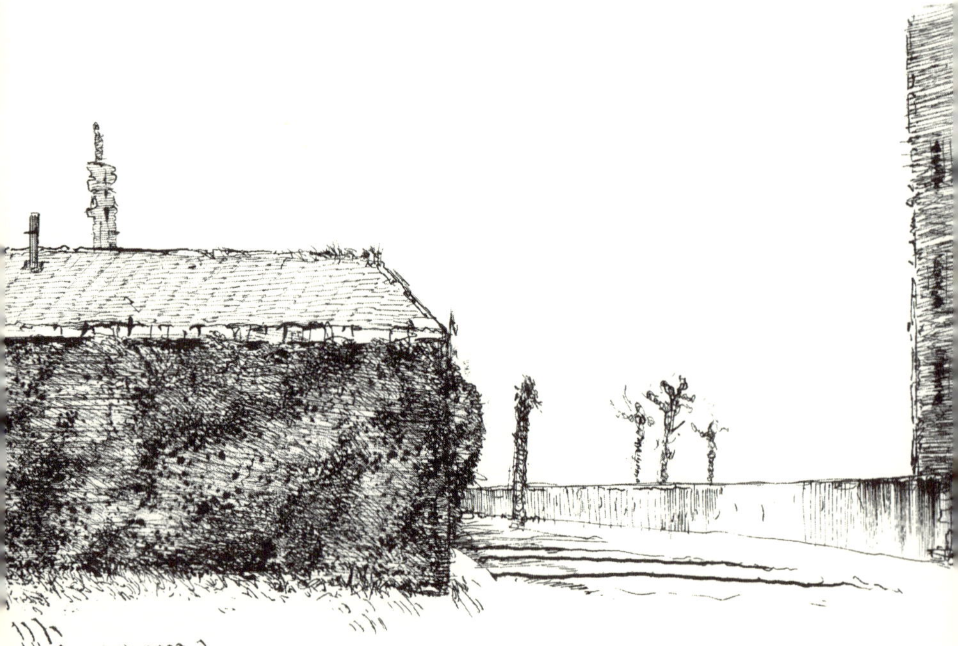